Student Support Materials for AQA

AS Geography

Unit 1

Physical and Human Geography

Authors: Philip Banks and Ruth Ward
Series Editor: David Redfern

Published by Collins Education
An imprint of HarperCollins Publishers
77-85 Fulham Palace Road
Hammersmith
London
W6 8JB

Browse the complete Collins Education catalogue at
www.collinseducation.com

10 9 8 7 6 5 4 3 2 1

ISBN 978-0-00-741570-0

British Library Cataloguing in Publication Data. A Catalogue record for this
publication is available from the British Library.

Commissioning Editor: Lucy McLoughlin
Project Manager: Lucien Jenkins
Design and typesetting: Hedgehog Publishing Ltd
Cover Design: Angela English
Index: Dr Laurence Errington
Production: Simon Moore
Printed and bound by L.E.G.O. S.p.A., Italy

Acknowledgements

Every effort has been made to contact the holders of copyright material, but if any have been inadvertently overlooked
the publishers will be pleased to make the necessary arrangements at the first opportunity.

p.26 Prince William Sound Science Center/www.pwssc.org; p.29 British Antarctic Survey/www.antarctica.ac.uk; p.29
bottom, © Collins Geo; p.34 © Collins Geo; p.41 © hammondovi/istockphoto.com; p.42 © Collins Geo; p.47 © Mike
Norton/istockphoto.com; p.48 © Collins Geo; p.50 © Collins Geo, ©National Oceanic and Atmospheric Administration/
www.noaa.gov; p.53 © Collins Geo;p.56 © Crown/www.statistics.gov.uk; p.57 © Crown, Census 2000/www.statistics.gov.
uk; p.58 © U.S. Census Bureau/www.census.gov; p.60 © Crown/www.statistics.gov.uk; p.63 © Andy Farrer/shutterstock.
com; p.66 © Collins Geo;p.71 © European Commission/ec.europa.eu; p.74 © Hector Conesa/shutterstock.com; p.77
© Christopher Furlong/gettyimages.co.uk, © Crown/www.decc.gov.uk; p.80 © Christopher Furlong/gettyimages.
co.uk; p.82 © Pelamis WavePower Ltd/www.pelamiswave.com, © Collins Geo; p.83 © Sjoerd van der Wal/istockphoto.
com, © EIA International Energy Annual 2006/www.eia.doe.gov; p.84 © Hanham Hall/www.hanhamhall.co.uk; p.85
© graham heywood/istockphoto.com; p.86 © Collins Geo; p.87 © Collins Geo/World Health Organisation/www.who.
int; p.89 © Collins Geo/World Health Organisation/www.who.int; p.92 © Crown/www.statistics.gov.uk; p.93 © Crown/
www.statistics.gov.uk; p.95 © Crown/www.statistics.gov.uk; p.110 © Bill Lawson/shutterstock.com; p.121 © Collins Geo/
Center for Security Studies/BP Statistical Review/www.sta.ethz.ch; p.126 © Collins Geo/World Health Organisation/
www.who.int; p.127 © Collins Geo.

All other photos supplied by the authors

Contents

Drainage basins

Drainage basins are bounded by high land, beyond which any precipitation will fall into the adjacent drainage basin. Drainage basins can come in a variety of scales from a very small scale to continental (e.g. The Mississippi/Missouri/Ohio Basin).

The drainage basin hydrological cycle

This is the part of the hydrological cycle that starts when precipitation first lands on a surface and finishes when water leaves the drainage basin either by **evapotranspiration** or as a river enters the sea. The way in which the water travels through the system into the river determines how the river reacts.

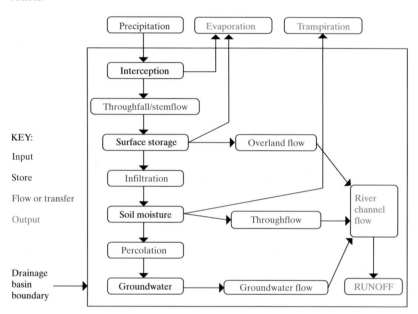

Fig 1
The drainage basin hydrological cycle

As water travels through the drainage basin it can stop, for a while, in a **store**. These water stores can be as follows:

- There can be **interception** on the leaves/branches of vegetation. Some vegetation is a better interception store than others. This can be due to the nature of the leaves (e.g. deciduous broad leaves or coniferous needles) and/or the density of the vegetation growth.
- On the surface, it usually appears in the form of puddles. While common in a man-made environment they are relatively rare in natural environments. Water usually disappears into the ground at a greater rate than it rains. Water can only build up on the surface after a long period of rain, an intense rainstorm, or on an impermeable surface (either man-made, e.g. an impacted footpath; or natural, e.g. a bare rock or frozen surface).

- Water can be stored in the vegetation. The amount that is stored depends on the type of vegetation and the time of year.
- In the soil.
- In the ground (rocks) beneath the surface. Some rocks are able to store a lot of water, especially if they are porous. These are called aquifers.
- Water is stored in the river channel itself.

Water travels between these stores in what are known as flows or transfers. These include the following:

- Water making its way from the leaves of trees to the ground. This drips/falls (**throughfall**) from one interception store to another until it eventually reaches the ground. Water also flows down the stems of grasses etc., and in very heavy storms it can flow straight down the trunks of trees. This is called **stemflow**.
- Water sinks into the soil by the process of **infiltration**. The speed at which this happens is called the infiltration rate. The infiltration rate is generally great enough to cope with the aggregate of direct precipitation and throughfall/stemflow, but if it is exceeded then water travels across the ground surface in **overland flow**. This can be fast-moving and large amounts of water can get to a river quickly.
- Some water is transpired through leaves.

When water gets into the soil it can travel towards the nearest river by **throughflow**. This tends to be much slower than overland flow. Generally speaking, the more vegetated an area, the faster the rate of throughflow because it is aided by root channels in the soil.

Water can **percolate** into the rocks below. The rate that this happens depends upon the rock type. Generally, permeable rocks allow a greater rate of percolation than impermeable ones. They also allow faster sideways movement through the rocks (**groundwater flow**).

All of these flows lead water to the nearest river (or deep **groundwater** store). The river then transfers water by channel flow. The amount of water that leaves the drainage basin in this way is called **runoff.**

The third output from the drainage basin is evaporation. This can take place from all stores.

Examiners' notes

You must:

- know the meaning of all the technical terms used in the drainage basin hydrological cycle
- be able to describe the cycle as a logical sequence
- understand how changes in the amount of water stored, and the rates of transfer, can affect the speed and quantity of water that reaches the river.

Essential notes

The drainage basin hydrological cycle is an open system. Although the relationship between the inputs and outputs can be very complex, it can be summed up by the equation: $P = Q + E + \Delta S$ where:

P is precipitation

Q is runoff (measured in m^3s^{-1} or CUMECS)

E is evapotranspiration

ΔS is the change in storage (in surface, soil, vegetation or the bedrock)

The storm hydrograph

Fig 2
The storm hydrograph

Essential notes

A hydrograph is a graph of river discharge against time. A storm hydrograph is the graph of the discharge of a river leading up to and following a storm or rainfall event. These graphs are important because they can predict how a river might respond to a rain storm. This can help in managing the river.

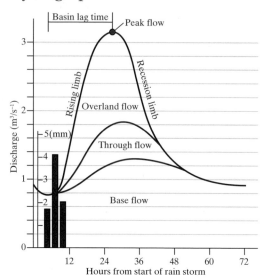

Examiners' notes

Storm hydrographs can be described in terms of:

- Rising limb
- Peak flow
- Lag time
- Recession limb
- Time taken to return to base flow.

The hydrograph in **fig 2** has a steep rising limb with a peak flow of 3.2 cumecs 21 hours after the peak rainfall (lag time). The recession limb is also steep and the river returns to base flow 72 hours after the onset of the storm.

Variables within the drainage basin can have an effect on the shape of the storm hydrograph.

The following diagrams show the effects of just four of these variables.

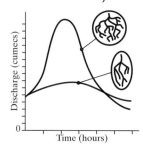

Fig 3
Influence of basin shape

Essential notes

Overland flow is the fastest movement of water to the river. Vegetated areas with established root channels allow fast throughflow and infiltration.

Water takes less time to reach the river in a round drainage basin than in an elongated one (**fig 3**).

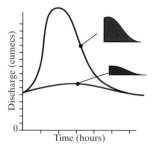

Fig 4
Influence of steepness

In steep-sided drainage basins (or the upper reaches of a river) water gets to the river more quickly than in an area of gentle slopes. (**fig 4**).

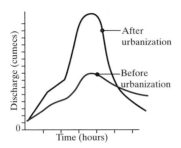

Fig 5
Influence of land use

The river itself can also be altered, e.g. to move the water rapidly away from the urban area (**fig 5**).

The growth of towns and cities has a major effect on the flow of rivers. Impermeable surfaces, shaped to get rid of water combined with a dense network of smooth drains, means that water gets to the river very quickly.

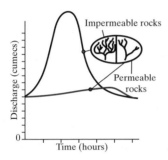

Fig 6
Influence of geology: differential hydrographs of impermeable and permeable rocks

Permeable rocks allow infiltration to occur, which slows down the rate of transfer of water to the river as well as the total amount of water. Impermeable rocks lead to more overland flow and faster transfer of water to the river (**fig 6**).

Other factors affecting the shape of a hydrograph are:

- **Intensity of storm:** The more intense it is, the more likely the infiltration rate will be exceeded and there will be overland flow.
- **The type of vegetation:** (see note on p. 5).

When water is transferred to a river quickly the resultant hydrograph is described as flashy. This means that the river responds very quickly to the storm. This often leads to flooding.

The long profile – changing processes

As you move from the source to the mouth the processes that take place in the river change.

Types of river erosion

Hydraulic action is the force of air and water on the sides of rivers and in cracks. It includes:

- **Evorsion:** the direct force of flowing water. This is most effective in turbulent flow.
- **Cavitation:** In this process bubbles form in flowing water. These bubbles can implode next to or within cracks in the bank. They then evict tiny jets of water that can move at up to 130m/sec. This can damage solid rock.

Hydraulic action is most commonly seen on the outside of meanders where it undercuts and causes collapse.

Abrasion is the wearing away of the bank and bed by the load of the river. It is the mechanical impact of debris as it is picked up and moved by the force of the moving water on the bed and banks. The effectiveness of the process depends upon the nature of the bedrock and the hardness and energy of the impacting pebbles. It increases as velocity increases. This forms potholes, and smoothes the bed of the river.

Solution (or corrosion) is the removal of chemical ions, especially calcium. The key factors in the rate of erosion are the geology of the bedrock, solute concentration of the stream water, and discharge and velocity.

Attrition is the wearing away of the load carried by the river. It usually involves particles/pebbles banging into one another and knocking off any angularity as well as hitting the bed.

Thus, in most rivers, the load decreases in size downstream as well as becoming more rounded.

Types of river transportation

The surplus energy of the river is used to carry the river's load. This is obtained in two ways: eroded material or material that has arrived by mass movement from the sides of the river.

Suspension is where the particles are carried within the flow of the river without touching the river bed. This is usually very fine material. Although each individual grain is small, they make the largest contribution to the river's load.

Saltation is where the particle moves from the river bed to the water in quick continuous repeated cycles. It entails the small stones bouncing along the river bed. As each one lands, it dislodges more pebbles which are then moved along in the flowing water.

Traction is where the load rolls and bounces along the river bed. In times of normal flow this will be sand, but when the river floods this can be rocks and boulders.

Essential notes

Work done by a river

- A river is a moving mass of water. This means that it has kinetic energy.
- Kinetic energy $KE = \frac{1}{2}mv^2$ where m is the mass of water and v is the velocity.
- An increase in the mass or velocity of water in a river (i.e. the discharge Q) will give the river more energy.
- A body that has energy is able to do work.

This work includes erosion and transportation. When a river loses energy it deposits its load.

Upper course	Middle course	Lower course
Erosion:	Erosion:	Erosion:
Abrasion with some hydraulic action	Mainly hydraulic action	Reduced but with some hydraulic action on outside of bends
Mostly vertical erosion	Less vertical erosion and more lateral erosion	
Transportation:	Transportation:	Transportation:
The load size varies a great deal. Large boulders are moved in times of high discharge and they roll and bounce their way downstream, banging away at the river bed.	The much smaller load size is moved along the river bed by rolling (**traction**) or bouncing (**saltation**). Finer material is moved in suspension during floods.	Sand is moved along the river bed by traction and fine material (silt and clay) is moved in suspension even when the river is not in flood.
Deposition:	Deposition:	Deposition:
All the coarse material stays where it is when a river reduces its discharge.	Deposition of sand and gravel occurs on the insides of meanders. Some flood plain deposits occur when the river overflows.	This consists of fine silts and clays, both on the river bed and on flood plains. Coarser material is dropped to form levees in times of flood.

Examiners' notes

Abrasion and attrition are commonly confused. Abrasion wears away the bed and the banks of a river; attrition is where the load of the river gets smaller.

Essential notes

Total sediment load = dissolved load + suspended load + bed load + floatation load

Essential notes

The Hjulstrom curve is an attempt to relate the work done by a river to its velocity. It does not take into account any effects of turbulence within the river flow.

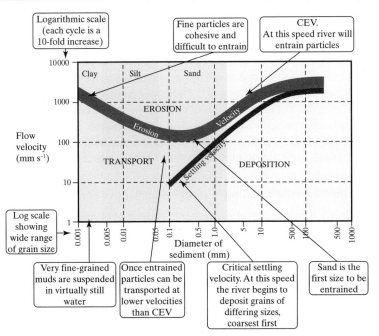

Fig 7
Hjulstrom's curve

Essential notes

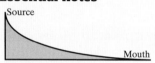

The graded profile of a river showing how it is smooth, concave and decreasing in gradient from source to mouth.

Valley profiles

The long profile

All rivers erode down to the **base level**, usually regarded as sea level. This is the lowest height that a land surface can be reduced to by a river.

In its journey from source to mouth a river generally has an increased velocity, discharge, load amount and efficiency. It has a decreased roughness, friction, turbulence and load size.

The idealized pattern is that the long profile is concave and has a smooth decrease in gradient as it flows from source to mouth. This is called the **graded profile**.

If the base level is changed in any way then rivers are encouraged to adjust their long profile accordingly. There are always imperfections in the long profile:

- There can be localized steepening indicated by waterfalls or rapids.
- There are also lengths where the gradient is reduced locally. These are often indicated by the presence of lakes.

Valley cross section

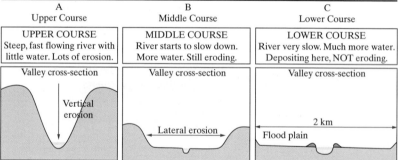

Valleys tend to be V-shaped in the upper reaches of a river but become increasingly wider with lower sides. The upper course is dominated by vertical erosion. Rocks and boulders scrape away at the base of the river creating landforms such as potholes. The sides are steep. As the river erodes downwards the sides collapse and rocks fall into the river to be used as abrasive tools until they are finally moved on down the river.

In the middle course there is a lot more lateral erosion. Meanders swing across the valley floor eroding the valley sides to form bluffs.

In the lower course the river uses most of its energy to transport load, so there is little erosion. When the river floods, the water leaving the channel immediately slows down. This loss of energy causes the river to deposit its load and cover the surrounding land with a veneer of mud and silt. This builds up to form a flood plain which stretches between the bluffs on either side of the valley.

The lower course is dominated by transport and deposition. The flood plains are wide and the bluffs very low.

Essential notes

A flood plain is not the direct result of erosion: a meandering river widens a valley floor; the flooding river deposits sediment on this wide valley floor.

A river's energy

In the upper reaches there is very little discharge. The velocity is low due to the roughness of the river bed. The river has mainly potential energy.

In physics, **potential energy** is the energy stored in a body or in a system due to its position in a force field. In the case of a river the force field is gravity. This dominates in the source area where the river is a long way above base level.

Further down the long profile the river is bigger and moving more quickly and so contains **kinetic energy**, where $KE = \frac{1}{2}mv^2$ and so is a function of the velocity and mass of the moving water.

Channel cross profile

The river channel changes from source to mouth. Near the source the channel is narrow, shallow and choked with boulders. At the mouth it is wide and deep, though interrupted by depositional islands. In the middle reaches of the river the channel can become asymmetrical. This is caused by **meanders** (see p 13).

The **wetted perimeter** is the length of the banks and bed in a cross section in contact with the moving water. In the upper course of a river this can be large in relation to its size. This is because of all the boulders in the channel.

The **hydraulic radius** is a measure of river-channel flow **efficiency**. It is defined as the ratio of the channel's cross-sectional area to its wetted perimeter.

$$(HR)\,Hydraulic\ radius = \frac{(CSV)\,cross\text{-}sectional\ area\ of\ the\ river}{(WP)\,wetted\ perimeter}$$

The higher the hydraulic radius, the more efficient the stream. This means that less energy is lost overcoming friction with the bed and bank of the river. This then allows the river to do more work. This work includes erosion and transport.

The greater the channel **roughness**, the greater the wetted perimeter. This means that an increasing length of the river's energy is lost in friction with the bank and bed. The river has less energy to erode and transport. Channel roughness is high in the upper reaches. Rivers only have enough energy to move the rocks and boulders when there are high flow levels.

Essential notes

Potential energy causes vertical erosion near the source.

Kinetic energy causes both vertical and lateral erosion.

Essential notes

Calculating hydraulic radius:

For a stream of 12 metres width and 1 metre depth:

The cross sectional area is 12m²

The wetted area is 14m

Hydraulic radius $= \dfrac{12}{14} = 0.86$

River landforms

Erosional landforms tend to be found in the upper parts of a river valley. They include: potholes, waterfalls and rapids.

Potholes are rounded depressions in the solid rock bed of a river. They are formed by a particular type of abrasion called **drilling**. Pebbles and gravel collect in a depression on the river bed. As the water flows past, it causes the pebbles to rotate in the hollow. Over time they drill down into the bedrock. More pebbles become trapped in the deepening hollow and the process continues.

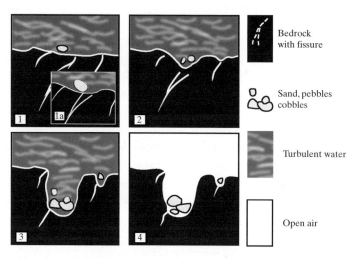

Bedrock with fissure

Sand, pebbles cobbles

Turbulent water

Open air

Fig 9
How potholes form

Waterfalls are vertical drops in the long profile; they are commonly caused by a sudden change in the geology caused either by faulting or by base level change.

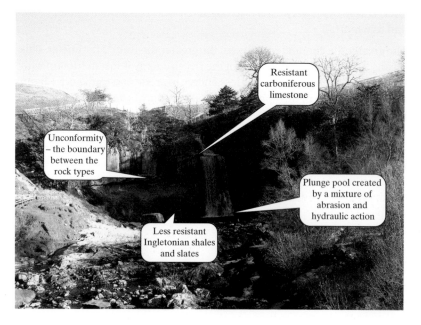

Resistant carboniferous limestone

Unconformity – the boundary between the rock types

Plunge pool created by a mixture of abrasion and hydraulic action

Less resistant Ingletonian shales and slates

Fig 10
A waterfall created by a change in geology –Thornton Force

The lip of the waterfall is undercut, causing collapse. This leads to the waterfall migrating upstream with a gorge being formed below the waterfall.

Rapids are steeper sections of the long profile characterized by a solid rock bed and very turbulent flow. They are often caused by changes in geology.

Meanders

Rivers with straight channels are rare. Even in the upper stage of a river it flows around interlocking spurs. In the middle and lower stages of rivers the river can become very sinuous, with **meanders** forming. Meanders are a combination of erosion and deposition. When a river is at its base flow, the main flow of water (the **thalweg**) can be seen to zig-zag down the channel between bars of sediment on opposing banks. The rivers form alternating deeper pools and shallower riffles. When the thalweg swings towards the bank it erodes by undercutting. Where there is slower flow deposition occurs. This makes the river bend more acutely.

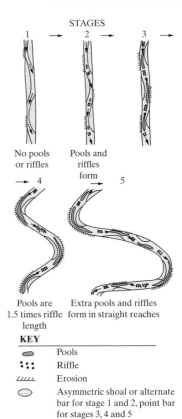

Once the river is no longer straight the movement of the thalweg downstream becomes like a giant corkscrew which swings from side to side of the channel as well as moving vertically. Where the thalweg is close to the banks and is moving downwards then undercutting of the bank occurs and river cliffs are formed. This exaggerates the shape of the river bend. Where the thalweg is rising, and on the inside of bends, deposition occurs, leading to a point bar.

When the outer part of the meander bend reaches the valley sides it erodes these to form bluffs. Eventually, the meanders migrate downstream slowly widening the valley floor.

When a river floods, it leaves a veneer of sediment on the valley floor to form a flood plain.

Fig 11
A meander on the river Dane, Cheshire, showing erosion of river cliff and deposition on point bar

Essential notes

Oxbow lakes are simply a result of over-exaggeration of meanders so that the meander neck is eroded to isolate the old meander. This eventually dries up and fills with sediment and vegetation.

This topic continues on the next two pages

Flood plains

Flood plains are flat areas of deposition close to a river channel.

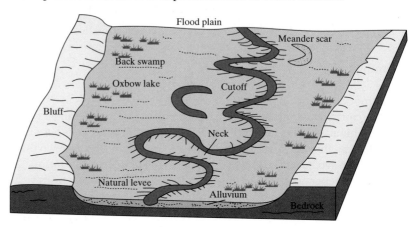

Adjacent to the channel many rivers have natural embankments called **levees**. These are formed during floods. As the sediment-charged river water leaves the channel it slows immediately and so deposits its coarsest load of gravel and pebbles. These levees act as a natural flood defence. As the levees build up, the river bed also gets sediment deposited and so the channel can be raised above the flood plain.

Deltas are formed when a river enters the sea. Two processes occur:

- The river slows down, loses competence and deposits sediment.
- The fresh river water mixes with the salty sea water and the sediment particles coagulate together in a process called **flocculation**.

As long as there is a greater rate of deposition than sediment removal there will be net deposition. The two most common types of delta are:

- Arcuate, e.g. the Nile delta.
- Bird's foot, e.g. the Mississippi delta.

Braided channels occur when a river is carrying large amounts of eroded sediment. This sediment is deposited in the channel as small islands (**eyots**) when the river loses competence. The two most common causes of this are:

- Energetic sediment-charged glacial meltwater streams flowing over a flat plain below the glacier.
- Fast-flowing rivers in a desert following a thunderstorm, which pick up loose debris but then redeposit it when the river dries up.

Process and impact of rejuvenation

Rejuvenation occurs when a river changes from being in equilibrium with its landscape to being dominated by erosion. The main causes of rejuvenation are:

- Uplift of the land following the melting of land-bound ice at the end of a glacial period–this tends to occur only where there has once been ice and so is localized.

- Uplift of land caused by local tectonic processes.
- Lowering of sea level caused by ice accumulating on land and so removing water from the oceans. This happens globally.

Knickpoints, river terraces and incised meanders

As a result of this increased difference between the height of the river and that of the sea, the river gains potential energy. This increases the river's ability to erode vertically. The landforms created because of this include knickpoints (and associated waterfalls and rapids), river terraces and incised meanders.

Knickpoints are sudden changes in river gradient. If there are a series of sea level changes then there are a series of steps.

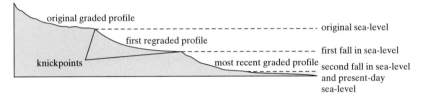

River terraces occur when a river cuts down into its flood plain to reach the new graded profile. This leaves the old floodplain as a terrace on the valley side.

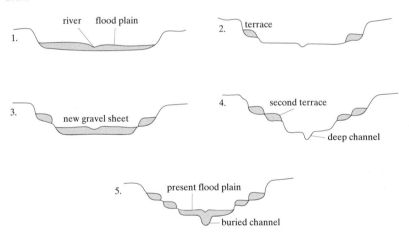

Incised meanders are the result of established meanders cutting vertically into the landscape. They come in two forms:

- Ingrown meanders occur when the vertical erosion is slow, allowing the meander to migrate within its newly developed flood plain. This produces asymmetrical valleys with steep cliffs on the outside of the bend.
- Entrenched meanders are caused by rapid vertical erosion creating a winding gorge.

Fig 13
The effect of rejuvenation on the long profile

Essential notes

River terraces are often paired, caused by successive sea level changes.

Fig 14
Formation of river terraces

Physical and human causes of flooding

A river flood occurs when the amount of river water is too great for the capacity of the channel. When this happens it either flows over the top of the bank onto the adjacent flood plain and/or backs-up in smaller tributaries which then overflow.

The causes of flooding can be divided into physical and human causes.

Physical causes

These are mainly climatological and include:

- Excessive rainfall occurring over a long period of time. This leads to soil saturation and, eventually, overland flow. This rapid movement of water to the channel causes it to fill rapidly.
- When rainfall is very intense it can be greater than the infiltration rate of the surface. Again, overland flow occurs. This can be exacerbated by having an impermeable surface (e.g. hard-baked desert surface; frozen ground; impermeable geology).
- Rapidly melting snow.
- Coastal storm surges.

Human causes

These include:

- Growth of urban areas, with impermeable surfaces which are often designed to shed water quickly (sloping roofs; cambered roads etc.) and high density of smooth storm drains.
- **Deforestation**: this removes the interception store which in turn reduces the amount of rain evaporated. The vegetation store has been removed and the soil has a lower infiltration rate. Rain can quickly fill up the soil store. This results in overland flow. The overland flow will lead to soil erosion, which in turn leads to excess sediment in a river which also leads to flooding.
- Failure of dams.

Areas at risk from flooding can be mapped. In England and Wales the Environment Agency is responsible for flood prediction and management. Its website issues general and specific warnings. Look up whether there are any flood warnings for the area in which you live.

Flood prediction is not very reliable. Much of it is based on historical data. The **recurrence interval** can be calculated and this tells us how often (in years) a flood of a particular magnitude will occur. The Environment Agency works on protecting settlements from a flood likely to recur once every hundred years. With climate change and more extreme weather, many of the calculations may now be flawed.

Impact of flooding

The effects of flooding can be classified into physical and human (economic and social) impacts.

Physical impacts can include:

- The area of land flooded.
- The amount of sediment deposited (or washed away).
- Any change to the river's course (e.g. the cutting off of a meander to produce an oxbow lake).

Human impacts include:

- Economic costs to householders and insurance companies.
- Economic impact on businesses and agriculture.
- Economic cost of organizing help by government and aid agencies.
- Social impacts such as deaths, homelessness, displacement of people.
- Social impact of health issues (lack of access to clean water, increase in mental illness).

Flood management strategies

These can be divided into hard engineering and soft engineering strategies.

Hard engineering requires that either something is constructed or that the landscape is changed. This includes dams, river straightening, levee construction or enhancement and diversion spillways. Many settlements in the UK that are based on major rivers include a combination of some of the above, e.g. York and Shrewsbury. The Mississippi valley is protected by straightening, levees and wing dykes. Los Angeles is protected from its river by channelling the Los Angeles river in efficient concrete-lined channels. Most of these are very expensive and so are only generally found in the developed world, protecting high value property.

Soft engineering includes forecasts and warnings, flood plain management, wetland conservation, river banks conservation.

Better forecasting in Bangladesh has helped reduce the death toll from flooding by giving people enough time to get to safety in the recently constructed flood shelters. Flood plain zoning, where only certain types of land use is allowed on land liable to flooding, does not prevent the flood but reduces the effects. Contour ploughing and afforestation reduce the amount of overland flow, slowing down the rate at which the precipitation enters a river. Wetland and river bank conservation allows water to be stored in areas where it actually benefits the environment by enhancing habitats.

River restoration is more about enhancing the environment than reducing flood risk. Nevertheless, when rivers are returned to their original state, floods may be more frequent but less catastrophic than those which occur in a channelized, dredged and embanked urban river.

Examiners' notes

The specification requires candidates to study the impacts of two recent flooding events in contrasting areas of the world. Use the same studies as the ones chosen opposite.

Examiners' notes

Not all dams are for flood management. The Three Gorges Dam produces electricity and stores water, but is also part of a hard engineering flood management strategy to prevent flooding in the Lower Yangtze river. The Hoover Dam in the USA, by contrast, is designed to provide electricity and store water for irrigation and domestic/industrial use but not to prevent flooding. Be careful in your choice of case studies for each of hard and soft engineering.

Distribution of cold environments

The distribution of cold environments is due to a combination of high latitude, high altitude and continentality, all of which contribute to cooling effects.

Current areas include: the ice cap of Antarctica and northern Greenland; the **periglacial** and **tundra** environments of northern Russia, northern Scandinavia, northern Canada, and high mountain areas of the high Andes, Rockies, Himalayas and Alps.

Types of glaciers

Ice sheet: covers a large area where ice flows outwards from the centre.
Ice cap: dome-shaped masses of ice which develop on high plateaus.
Piedmont glaciers: formed where valley ice spreads out as it reaches lower areas.
Valley glacier: where ice flows down a previously smaller (usually river) valley.

Warm/temperate/alpine glaciers: found in areas where temperatures are high enough to cause some summer melting. This allows the glaciers to advance in winter and retreat in summer. The meltwater reduces friction and lubricates the base, allowing the glacier to move more quickly. This allows more material to be transported and, therefore, more erosion and deposition occurs with these types of glacier.

Cold/polar glaciers: found in areas where the temperature rarely rises above freezing so there is little melting or movement and much less erosion, transport and deposition.

Ice movement

Compressing/compressional flow: where the gradient is low and velocity is low the ice crystals push together and compress so the ice becomes thicker and erosion is greater.
Extending/extensional flow: where the gradient increases and the velocity increases the ice becomes thinner and erosion is less.
Basal flow: where the pressure of the ice and increased friction melt the ice at the base allowing it to slide.
Surges: a sudden forward movement of a glacier caused by a sudden rise in the amount of meltwater.
Internal deformation: where the ice crystals all set themselves in line with the movement of the glacier and slide past each other. The surface moves faster than the internal ice causing cracks called crevasses to form.

Glacial budgets

Snow and avalanches are examples of *inputs* which occur in the **zone of accumulation**.

In the **zone of ablation** *outputs* occur including: evaporation, sublimation, meltwater, calving and moraine.

Transfer is the movement of ice stored in the upper part of the valley by processes of gravity and glacial flow, to the lower area where it melts (ablates).

Essential notes

Past glacial and periglacial environments include Britain and most of central western Europe, where lower latitudes and altitudes show the imprint of the last (Pleistocene) glaciation.

Essential notes

When there is an obstacle to ice movement, e.g. a hard band of rock, the ice compresses behind it causing greater pressure and melting. The ice then moves over the obstacle through basal slippage, and scours it, but the water then refreezes as the gradient and velocity increases.

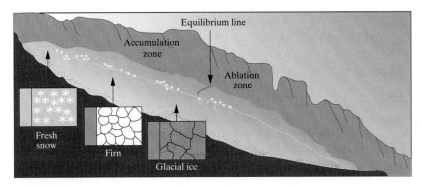

Fig 1
Glacial budget

An **equilibrium line** can be shown on a glacier where at any one time the amount of accumulation equals that of ablation. This is also called the **firn line**.

Glaciation processes: weathering

Freeze–thaw: where temperatures hover around freezing (above during the day and below at night) water in cracks in the rocks freezes at night, widening the crack by expansion. In the day more water collects in the crack which again freezes, widening the crack further. The rock then shatters into angular fragments which fall onto the ice and become tools for erosion by abrasion, or form mounds at the base of the slope forming **scree.**

Nivation: where physical and chemical weathering under a patch of snow cause the rock to disintegrate.

Glaciation processes: erosion

Plucking: where ice freezes onto the rock and sticks to it. As the mass of ice moves it drags on the rock pulling any loose fragments out.

Abrasion: sharp rock fragments carried by the ice embed themselves in the base of the ice. This is used to grind down the bedrock like sandpaper, making it smooth. It can leave scratches on the rock in the direction of ice movement, called **striations**.

Rotational slide: found where the hollow shape of the landscape, e.g at the base of a corrie, allows compressional flow of the ice, causing greater erosion and allowing the ice to rotate in the base of the hollow.

Transportation

Material from weathering and erosion can be carried by the ice on the surface, as supraglacial debris; within the ice, as englacial debris; at the base of the ice, as subglacial debris.

Deposition

Deposition occurs when the carrying capacity of the ice decreases because the gradient decreases, the velocity of the glacier decreases, or more material has to be transported. The ice leaves behind the material it can no longer carry. Material deposited by ice is called **till** or **boulder clay**. It is unsorted and angular. Ice deposition is either lodgement till, material left by moving ice, e.g. drumlins; or ablation till, material left when the ice starts to melt, e.g. terminal moraine. Deposition also results from meltwater.

Essential notes

Glaciers usually have a positive balance in winter when more snow accumulates and a negative balance in summer when there is more ablation due to higher temperatures.

Examiners' notes

You may be asked to identify sediment type and explain how you know whether it was left under the ice or by meltwater. Remember, unsorted angular material is left under the ice whereas sorted and less angular material is left by glacial meltwater.

Landforms and features of glacial areas

Features of glacial erosion

Corries (also known as cirques, cwms, coires) are deep armchair-shaped hollows high up on a mountainside. They are often north- or northeast-facing in the northern hemisphere, as this direction will receive the least sunlight and coldest winds, causing the snow to stay longer. Their size varies but they are often around 0.5 km in diameter with a steep back wall. At first the hollow is deepened by nivation, and then, as the ice accumulates, by rotational slide enhancing the abrasion process due to increased pressure. Ice pulls away from the back wall, plucking rocks already loosened by freeze-thaw weathering.

Where the pressure and erosion are lower at the front edge of the hollow there may be deposition of moraine at the lip of the corrie, which allows water to accumulate behind it forming a corrie lake or corrie tarn.

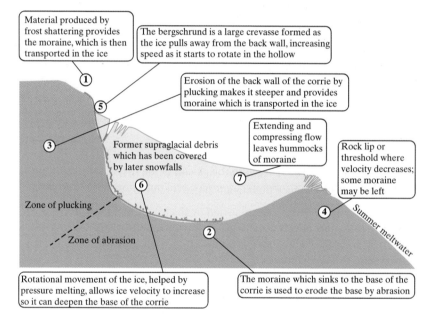

Fig 2
Corrie formation

Arêtes form where corries form back to back. The two steep back walls form a narrow, sharp ridge.

Pyramidal peaks form where three corries develop on a mountain. The back walls converge to form a triangular-shaped peak.

Glacial troughs develop where glaciers flow into river valleys. They widen and deepen the original valley making it steep-sided with a wide flat base (like a capital letter U). Glaciers tend to straighten the valley, cutting off spurs and leaving cliffs called **truncated spurs**. At the upper end of the valley, where the glacier has entered the valley from the corries above, there is often a steep wall called the **trough end**. Glacial flow is uneven, and where compressing flow has overdeepened a section of the valley, or where there is softer rock which is more easily eroded, it forms a rock basin which often fills with water forming a **ribbon lake**.

Hanging valleys form where ice in a tributary valley cannot erode effectively because its movement is blocked by ice in the main valley; it therefore remains higher and smaller than the main glacial trough (hanging above it). Once the ice has retreated water is released from the hanging valley as a waterfall into the main valley below.

Roches moutonnées form where a glacier moves over a band of harder rock and smoothes the upstream side by abrasion; there are often **striations** (scratches on the bare rock surface made by pieces of debris carried in the ice) showing the direction of the glacier's movement. As the glacier spills over the top of the obstruction it removes the loose rocks by plucking, leaving a jagged edge on the downstream side.

Features of areas of glacial deposition

Moraine is the name given to any material left by ice. It is of mixed size, unsorted and angular debris.

Terminal moraine is found where the glacier **snout** ended. It marks the point where ablation and accumulation were in balance for a long period of time.

Lateral moraine is moraine produced at the side of the glacier, having rolled there after falling on top of the ice or having fallen onto the side from frost shattering of the valley sides.

Medial moraine is found at the confluence of two glaciers, where two lateral moraines merged to form a moraine down the middle of the main glacier.

Ground moraine is formed beneath the glacier or ice sheet. Some is ground up into fine clay but a number of larger pieces of debris are mixed up with it, so it is often called **boulder clay** or **till**.

Push moraine is formed where ice has re-advanced down the valley and pushed materials ahead of it and left a moraine similar in shape to a terminal moraine. Many of the stones will have been pushed upwards.

Recessional moraine is formed where the ice has retreated up–valley from the terminal moraine and left a new pile of unsorted debris.

A **drumlin** is an elongated oval-shaped mound of unsorted till up to about 50m high and around 1 000m long, in a lowland valley or, more commonly, on the plains. The ice slows slightly if it exceeds its carrying capacity and drops some of the material it is carrying. It then picks up some of the material again and smoothes over the debris, forming a steep stoss end pointing up valley and a long gentle lee slope facing down–valley. They are often found in groups or swarms, where the landscape is described as 'basket of eggs topography', e.g. Strangford Lough.

Erratics are large rocks which have travelled on and in ice sheets and glaciers and been deposited a long way from their origin, sometimes thousands of kilometres.

Examiners' notes

When examination questions ask for features produced by glacial erosion make sure you don't write about deposition or fluvioglacial features instead, as this will cause you to lose marks.

Examiners' notes

You must ensure that you have examples of glacial erosion features. You could use North Wales with Cwm Idwal as an example of a corrie with a corrie tarn, the Nant Ffrancon glacial trough below it with truncated spurs several hanging valleys and a roche moutonnée.

Examiners' notes

Make sure that you can give named examples of the features of cold environments. This will help you to raise your grade in an exam. It is often particularly useful to start with learning the names of a number of different features which will be found in the same area, e.g. north Wales.

Fluvioglaciation and periglaciation

Features of fluvio-glacial deposition

Sandur (outwash plains) are large areas of material washed out of the ice by glacial meltwater streams. These streams carry a lot of debris in braided channels which leave the largest deposits nearest the ice front and carry finer particles further across the plain. The deposits are also affected by seasonal melting and appear in layers, showing the larger deposits occurring each spring with the increased meltwater. These deposits are less angular than those left by the ice itself, and are sorted by the water, leaving deposits over a wide area, e.g. south Iceland.

Essential notes

Make sure you can distinguish between kame terraces, which have sorted material as they are left by meltwater, and lateral moraines, which have unsorted material.

Fig 3
View of the sandur of Southern Iceland

Eskers are long winding sandy ridges (often several km long) formed from sediments left by meltwater streams flowing on the ice surface, within the ice, or at the base of the glaciers.

Kames are formed where cracks in the ice fill with sediment. When the ice melts the sediment falls to form a mound of sorted coarse sands and gravels. They can also form as deltas, where meltwater from the ice flows into a lake dammed up behind the terminal moraine down valley. These lakes leave large amounts of sediment behind, with the layered deposits reflecting the seasonal flow of meltwater into the lakes. These deposits are called **varves**.

Kame terraces develop where the sediment collects from streams or lakes which occur between the valley side and the glacier, and a long ridge develops.

Kettle holes often develop in the outwash plains. They occur where large chunks of residual ice have been buried beneath lake sediment, which protects them from heat and prevents them from melting for a long time. When they eventually melt they leave a large depression in the land surface which often forms a **kettle lake** when filled with water, or a marshy hollow.

Periglaciation

If soil stays frozen for two years **permafrost** will develop. However, in many areas the surface layers melt in the summer, thawing from the surface downwards forming the active layer.

Continuous permafrost: there is hardly any melting of the surface layer because the temperature rarely rises above freezing. The soil is frozen to a depth of up to 1.5km.

Discontinuous permafrost: the permafrost is only up to 35m deep and the surface melts in summer. Rivers and lakes causes the permafrost to be absent around them due to their 'warming' effect.

Sporadic permafrost: this is where the temperatures stay close to freezing and the permafrost is only found in cold spots.

Patterned ground

Patterned ground is caused by the growth and expansion of ice lenses, which force stones up to the surface by **frost heave** in two ways:

- **Frost pull**: during the winter soils freeze downwards from the surface, reaching individual stones, which are pulled upwards by the vertical expansion of the frozen soil above them. The empty space left beneath is filled with loose unfrozen soil, so the stone is prevented from moving back when the soil below freezes.
- **Frost push**: stones are pushed towards the surface due to the pressure of ice growing beneath them. This occurs because stones become colder more quickly than fine-grained soil, so ice will form first directly below stones. Stones also warm up more quickly (lower specific heat), so in the summer thaw the ice in the soil around the stone melts first, allowing wet sediment to slump and fill the space beneath the stone. This prevents it from sinking back into its original position.

Where the temperatures often hover around freezing, frost heave is at its maximum and larger stones are rolled down the mounds to form **stone polygons**. Where the slope is slightly steeper these become elongated to form **stone stripes**.

Ice wedges

Ice wedges form where contraction of the soil in winter opens cracks in the surface. During the summer thaw, meltwater and sediment fill the crack. The water freezes in winter and expands, widening the crack so that more water and sediment fills it the next summer. Over several years the crack forms a wedge of ice and sediment known as an ice wedge up to 1m wide. They often form polygonal shapes on the surface known as ice wedge polygons.

Screes

Screes form due to frost-shattered material depositing and building up at the foot of slopes. The stones lie at a constant angle (called the angle of repose) until dislodged by one stone or foot print, and then the slope becomes unstable and moves until again settling at the angle of repose. The larger boulders fall furthest down the slope and the smaller stones fill in behind.

Examiners' notes

The processes of frost pull and push explain many features of the periglacial landscape.

Examiners' notes

Make sure that you know the difference between ice wedge polygons (made from sediment) and stone polygons (shapes made from stones) and that you can describe them accurately.

☞ This topic continues on the next two pages

Pingos

These are dome-shaped features up to 50m high. There are two theories for their formation:

- The East Greenland or open system type where the permafrost layer is thin and free water is pushed up by hydraulic pressure as the active layer re-freezes, thereby lifting the sediments above it (**fig 4**).
- The Mackenzie/closed system type which involves less freezing of the soil around small lakes due to the water providing better insulation for the soil around the lake, as in the Mackenzie Basin area of Canada.

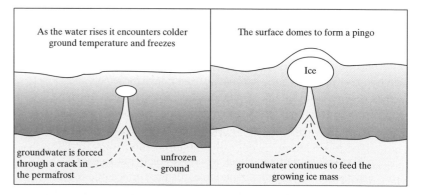

Fig 4
Diagrams to show the open system theory of pingo formation

Essential notes

A talik is a layer of sediment that has thawed.

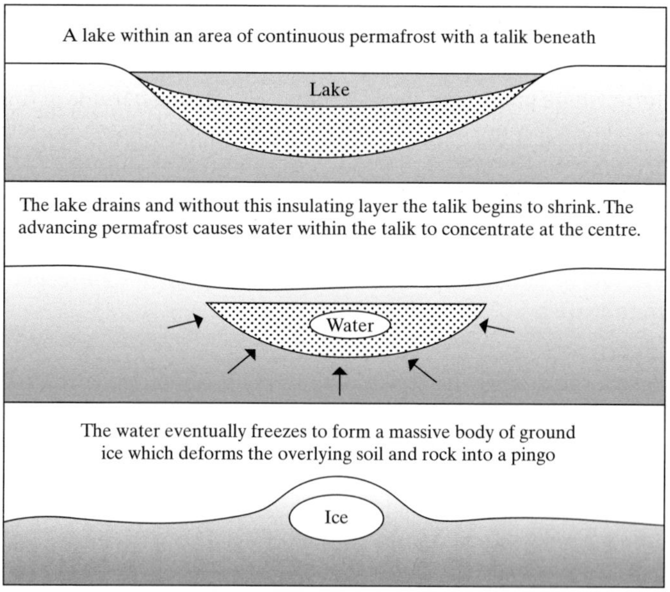

A lake within an area of continuous permafrost with a talik beneath

Lake

The lake drains and without this insulating layer the talik begins to shrink. The advancing permafrost causes water within the talik to concentrate at the centre.

Water

The water eventually freezes to form a massive body of ground ice which deforms the overlying soil and rock into a pingo

Ice

Fig 5
Diagrams to show the closed system theory of pingo formation

Blockfields (Felsenmeer)

These are larger blocks of stone released by frost shattering which slowly spread across the flat plains forming a field or sea of rocks.

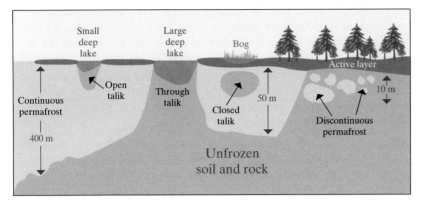

Fig 6
Types of permafrost

Solifluction lobes

In areas where there is discontinuous permafrost the subsoil does not thaw in summer so surface meltwater cannot percolate into the rock beneath. The soil becomes saturated and starts to flow downhill on even the gentlest of slopes. Reduced friction between particles due to the water content, and a lack of vegetation to hold the soil together, allow the soil to move, leaving tongue-like protrusions. Where the slope is steeper on the valley sides, **solifluction terracettes** form.

Nivation hollows

These form where patches of snow do not melt for long periods of time, usually because they lie in a small hollow on a north-facing slope. Freeze-thaw weathering beneath the snow patch, combined with the downslope movement of sediment out of the hollow during the summer by meltwater, causes deepening by erosion.

Essential notes

Erosion and weathering are often confused. Erosion involves movement by ice, water, wind or the sea. Weathering happens in situ – as the rock sits there.

Essential notes

Estimated loss of wildlife following the Exxon spill:

- 250000 seabirds
- 2800 sea otters
- 300 harbour seals
- 250 bald eagles
- 22 killer whales

People and cold environments

There are several key ideas which should be mentioned when writing about extreme environments. Clearly, the *survival* of people in extreme environments relies on people living in *balance* with the environment, using it in *sustainable* ways. However, this is often in conflict with the need for *exploitation* of minerals found here, which in turn can improve the *standard of living* of the local people by providing paid jobs and bringing in modern communications and technology. There has also been a growth in *tourism* which can help to improve the economy. On the other hand, this can also cause a loss of *culture* and involves issues of *habitat protection* in what are often *wilderness* areas.

Alaska

Alaska has vast reserves of oil and gas. It was first found around Prudhoe Bay in the north, which was inaccessible to ships due to pack ice. A pipeline needed to be built to the ice-free port of Valdez on the south coast of Alaska. It was built on insulated legs so that the warmed oil (the oil is warmed so that it does not freeze) will not melt the permafrost and cause the pipeline to sink and break, and was raised on stilts to avoid blocking the Caribou migration route. It also zig-zags to avoid breaking due to ground movement by either frost heave or earthquakes. Ships carrying oil here can cause damage to wildlife and the natural environment. The worst incident happened in March 1989, when the tanker *Exxon Valdez*, en route from Valdez, Alaska to Los Angeles, California, ran aground on Bligh Reef in Prince William Sound, Alaska. The vessel was travelling outside normal shipping lanes in an attempt to avoid ice. It spilled approximately 10.9 million gallons of Prudhoe Bay crude oil, which caused a huge oil slick to spread for over 1100 miles along the coastline, causing huge environmental damage and destruction of wildlife.

Buildings in this area of the tundra are insulated or raised above the ground with piles driven into the permafrost to avoid the ground warming up and developing **thermokarst**. **Utilidors** are used to carry water-heating and waste pipes so that they don't melt the permafrost and cause the buildings to sink. A new chilled gas pipeline is proposed to take gas from northern Alaska to Alberta in Canada, which will act as a distribution centre. The gas will be compressed and chilled before being sent down the large-diameter pipeline, which can be buried because it should not heat up or melt the permafrost. It will provide jobs and develop more local gas supplies within the American continent. On the other hand, the buildings for the workforce and factories required to maintain the flow of gas, plus all the building work, may well adversely affect the environment, disturbing caribou herds and vegetation.

The Alps

The Alps present an example of a high-altitude cold environment. There are conflicts between tourists and farming/settlement and even different tourist groups. Avalanches can be set off by skiing and snowboarding off piste. Some people argue that tourist hotels, cable cars and ski lifts ruin the landscape. The development of mountain sports and tourism in these remote areas has improved the transport network, and improved the economy by developing jobs in the tourist industry (in hotels, etc.), which has kept more people living in the area and prevented further rural depopulation. However, many people feel that the fragile environment has been damaged, with the loss of rare plants such as orchids and birds such as the golden eagle.

Sami reindeer herders

The Sami people originally lived in northern Scandinavia and Russia's Kola Peninsula. Their population is estimated at 60000. They have their own language and culture. Their traditional activity is reindeer herding. Which provides everything they need.

The main commercial product is meat, although cured reindeer leather is still being used to make boots and handbags. Sami art objects and handicrafts are sold to tourists.

In August the grazing becomes less plentiful so the reindeer are moved towards the lower fells, just below the tree line. All reindeer meat for commercial sale must be slaughtered under controlled conditions, so enclosures are often located next to roads, for easy journeys by road to the slaughterhouse.

After the mating season in October, the Sami gather the reindeer before driving them in November or December to winter pastures in the coniferous forest. In the north these migrations may be 300–400km long. In the winter pastures lichen from old trees is an essential part of the reindeer diet, but due to modern forestry it is in short supply. Sometimes the reindeer are kept in enclosures and are fed hay and other commercial fodder during the winter.

Mechanised forestry, hydroelectric power plants and mining operations have threatened the traditional Sami occupations of reindeer breeding, hunting and fishing. Snow scooters have replaced the reindeer sleighs and skis. It is no longer a nomadic life, and many now live in urban areas. Most Sami children attend ordinary schools. There has been a decline in their common culture and language and a rise in occupational illnesses such as lifting- and vibration-related injuries.

There are conflicts regarding Sami land use. Forest owners regard reindeer as a threat to their newly planted forest. There are complaints about reindeer eating plants in people's gardens and creating a traffic hazard.

Some Sami are now considering old methods again: Icelandic horses have been imported to replace some motorized vehicles. This could revitalize the unique cultural elements of reindeer farming, the close contact with animals and nature.

The Sami have their own parliament in Norway and in Sweden and the Nordic Sami Council supports their culture. They have achieved new linguistic rights as well as state support for a variety of cultural activities.

Examiners' notes

Be careful to choose the right examples to illustrate your answers. You can use the Sami of northern Norway, and the areas of Alaska and northern Canada as examples of present-day periglacial/tundra environments. The high Alps, high Himalayas and Antarctica are covered by permanent snow and ice and are therefore glacial and ice-covered environments.

Examiners' notes

Questions often require a discussion. It would be useful to be able to argue both for and against the idea that human survival has been successful and is sustainable using these case studies. Make a list of the main points and revise them.

Antarctica

Antarctica is a wilderness area protected by the Antarctic Treaty. This environment is fragile because of the short food chains in the Southern Ocean **food web**.

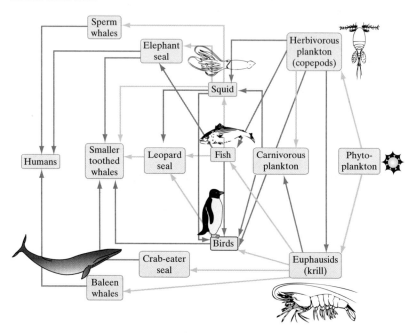

Fig 7
The Southern Ocean food web showing the short food chains and the importance of keeping the sea free from pollution

Essential notes

Keep your notes up to date by visiting the following websites to add to your case studies:

For Antarctica, see:
- www.antarctica.gov.au (for information on laws and treaties)
- www.state.gov/g/oes/ rls/rpts/ant/ (for the Handbook of the Antarctic Treaty)
- www.antartica.ac.uk (for the British Antarctic Survey)

For tundra, see:
- http://www.bbc.co.uk/ tribe/tribes/nenets/index. shtml (following a BBC documentary on Siberia and the Nenets).

Remember the content of websites changes over time.

The Antarctic Treaty System (ATS) is a complex of arrangements designed to ensure 'in the interests of all mankind that Antarctica shall continue forever to be used exclusively for peaceful purposes and shall not become the scene or object of international discord'. It prohibits 'any measures of a military nature' but does 'not prevent the use of military personnel or equipment for scientific research or for any other peaceful purpose'. The Treaty provides for 'freedom of scientific investigation in Antarctica', and 'promote[s] international cooperation in scientific investigation'. The original signatories included the governments of Argentina, Australia, Belgium, Chile, France, Japan, New Zealand, Norway, the Union of South Africa, Russia, the United Kingdom and the USA. More recent appendices (1991) protect the environment, ensuring that waste is removed and that tourist numbers are limited. Mineral exploration and exploitation is not permitted.

Whaling for meat, oil and whalebone caused whaling stations to be set up on South Georgia for meat processing. As whales, especially the blue whale, began to die out, many countries stopped the trade. Fishing is now the main economic use of the area; krill stocks are crucial for this, but they are fished by Russian and Japanese trawlers. If the krill disappear then the whole of the food chain will collapse. Seal hunting had already almost wiped out the seal population here and fish stocks are depleted. The future of the Antarctic depends on conservation of resources, especially those of the ocean. The development of small-scale tourism began in Antarctica in the 1950s, with commercial tour operators providing passenger ships.

The first specially designed, ice-strengthened cruise ship, the *Lindblad Explorer*, visited in 1969. Since then, the industry has grown considerably, with numbers of tourists increasing from under 9,000 in 1992/93 to over 46,000 in 2007/08.

Tourists come to see the wildlife here and this activity is small-scale, so could be argued to be sustainable.

However, the summer is the breeding season for most of the wildlife they visit and any disturbance could upset the balance. There is also pressure on the landing sites which receive most tourists, especially the old whaling stations, and historic sites such as McMurdo Sound where the original huts from Scott's expedition are found.

There are many resources as yet undeveloped in Antarctica, including oil, coal and many metals. In the future there will be increased pressure to develop these resources, especially as present-day fields begin to run out. Global warming may well open up the fringe areas of Antarctica for settlement, putting the Treaty under threat.

Essential notes

All tour operators providing visits to Antarctica are members of the International Association of Antarctica Tour Operators (IAATO), which seeks to ensure that tourism in Antarctica is conducted in an environmentally friendly way. The British Antarctic Survey welcomes a small number of visits to its stations and groups are given a guided tour of the facilities, where they have the opportunity to learn about the scientific research undertaken by BAS. Visits to Bird Island on South Georgia are not permitted as it is a Site of Special Scientific Interest (SSSI). Source: BAS website.

Fig 8
Antarctica

Essential notes

Waves at sea follow an orbital movement and objects do not travel forward. Objects are moved by tides and currents. When the wave reaches shallow water, the movement of the base of the wave is slowed by friction with the sea bed, the wave spills forward as a breaker moving objects forward with it.

Examiners' notes

Make sure you know the difference between the effects of these two types of waves on the coast. You can work out whether erosion or deposition is dominant by counting the number of waves per minute!

Essential notes

Some of the highest tidal ranges in the world are found on the west coast of the UK, causing tidal bores. At the Severn estuary, the tide races into a quickly narrowing channel generating a wave over 1m (sometimes up to 4m) high as it runs upriver, disturbing the river bank wildlife ahead of it. The Severn bore has become a tourist attraction, with surfers riding on it. Find out more at: www.severn-bore. co.uk

Coastal systems and processes

The coastline has several identifiable zones:

- **Backshore** – above the high tide mark (except for spring tides and storm waves);
- **Foreshore** – the inter-tidal zone;
- **Inshore/Nearshore** – just below the low water mark;
- **Offshore** – beyond the main action of the waves.

Waves

Waves are caused by the wind blowing over the surface of the sea. Wave energy is controlled by wind force and direction and duration of wind. **Fetch** is the distance over which the wind has blown. Waves break and rush up the beach as **swash** and return down the beach as **backwash**.

Constructive waves construct or build beaches. They have longer wavelengths, lower height, and are less frequent (6–8 per minute). Swash is greater than backwash so constructive waves add to beach materials, giving rise to a gently sloping beach.

Destructive waves have a steeper gradient, are more frequent (10–14 per minute), a shorter wavelength and greater height. The backwash is greater than the swash so that sediment is dragged offshore.

Tides are caused by the gravitational pull of the moon and less so the sun, usually causing two high tides and two low tides each day. (The interval between each high tide is 12 hours 25 minutes.)

Spring tides occur when the gravitational pull is strongest because the sun, moon and earth are in a straight line; this happens twice a lunar month. It causes the high tide to be at it highest and the low tide at its lowest point.

Neap tides happen during the alternate weeks in the lunar month when the earth, moon and sun form a right angle, lessening the gravitational pull and giving a lower tidal range.

Tidal range refers to the difference between the height of the high and low tides. Where there is a larger difference, as around the west coast of Britain, it is said to be **macrotidal**; erosion is greater and **tidal bores** can develop in estuaries.

Storm surges occur where water levels are much higher than those of high tide and can cause flooding. They occur in places where the sea area narrows (e.g. the southern part of the North Sea), when several factors combine:

- Very low atmospheric pressure raising the sea surface.
- Very high spring tides.
- Strong winds with a long fetch producing storm waves.
- Where the sea area narrows e.g., the southern part of the North Sea.

Sediment sources come from rivers, the sea bed, erosion of the coastline, shell material, and movement of materials along the coastline.

Sediment cells are distinct areas of coast separated by deep water or headlands, within which material is moved but the sediment inputs and outputs are in balance.

Coastal processes: erosion

Marine erosion refers to the way in which the waves erode coastlines.

Abrasion (corrasion) is where material carried by the waves is used as ammunition to wear away the rocks, as it is thrown against them repeatedly by each wave.

Solution (corrosion) involves the dissolving of rocks by sea water, especially limestones.

Attrition is the process by which rocks are broken down into smaller and more rounded particles, which are then used in abrasion.

Hydraulic action is where a wave breaking against rocks traps air into cracks in the rock under pressure which is released suddenly as the wave retreats. This causes stress in the rock which develops more cracks, allowing the rock to break up more easily.

The rate of coastal erosion is governed by several factors:
- **Geology**: harder rock, e.g. granite, is more difficult to erode than softer material like boulder clay. Hard rocks can be eroded along joints or cracks, and those like limestone are prone to solution. The structure and dip of the rocks also affect erosion.
- **Coastal shape**: softer rock is eroded to form bays, with the harder rocks forming headlands.
- **Wave steepness**: steeper high energy waves have more power to erode.
- **Fetch**: waves which have travelled a long distance have more energy.
- **Beaches**: these absorb some of the waves' energy and protect the coastline. Pebble beaches dissipate energy from steep waves through friction and percolation, allowing the beach to trap more sediment.
- **Human developments**: sand and pebble extraction from beaches for use as building materials weakens the coast's protection and can lead to erosion. Sea walls, groynes and other coastal protection schemes may help to protect an area from erosion, but can also increase erosion further along the coast. The building of quays and breakwaters can also change the movement of material along a section of coast. Developments on the top of cliffs can increase runoff and cause instability and cliff failure.

Coastal processes: transportation

Material is moved by:
- **Traction** in the breaking waves.
- **Swash and backwash:** materials are moved up the beach by swash and back down the beach by backwash.
- **Longshore drift:** material is moved along the shoreline. Swash moves up the beach at an angle but the backwash is at right angles to the beach. This results in material zigzagging its way along the beach in the direction of the prevailing wind.

Coastal processes: deposition

This occurs wherever the wave velocity is lower and swash is greater than backwash. Fine dry sand is often then moved by wind action to form sand dunes.

Examiners' notes

Ensure you know the difference between corrasion and corrosion, and are careful with spelling as these are sometimes confused.

Coastal landforms of erosion

Landforms of erosion

Headlands and bays: As waves approach the coast they become more parallel to the line of the coast, losing velocity and slowing down where the water is shallow and speeding up where it is deeper. Waves reach the shallow water off the headlands first, as high steep destructive waves, causing erosion here. The waves bend into the bays with lower levels of energy causing more deposition. This is called wave refraction.

Fig 1
The impact of wave refraction on headlands and bays

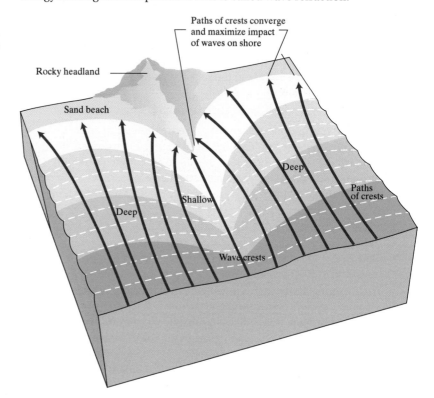

Essential notes

Blow holes are often called gloups after the noise made by the sea pushing air inside them at high tide, e.g. near Rhoscolyn on Anglesey.

Blow holes form where waves open up a joint or crack in the cliff face to form a more steep-sided inlet or geo. If this inlet is widened to become a small cave, a crack at the back of the cave may open up like a chimney to the surface, creating a hole at the top of the cliff above.

Caves, **arches** and **stacks**: where a cave is created on a headland and is eroded back into the headland it sometimes meets a cave which is being similarly eroded on the other side of the headland. The back wall separating the caves weakens and eventually the sea pushes through forming an arch. The sea is now able to splash under the arch further weakening it until eventually the arch roof collapses leaving the seaward side of it as a separate island called a stack. Over time the stack will be eroded to form a **stump**.

Fig 2
Dyrhólaey arch and stacks, Iceland

Cliffs and wave-cut platforms: In the tidal zone the base of a cliff will be eroded faster than the rock above. A wave-cut notch develops here and the other rocks overhang. Gravity causes the overlying rocks to fall and the cliff line retreats, leaving the remnants of the rocks of the original cliff line as an almost flat (less than 4°) base called the wave-cut platform. The larger the platform the less energy the waves have to erode the cliff further so a wave-cut platform acts as a cliff protector.

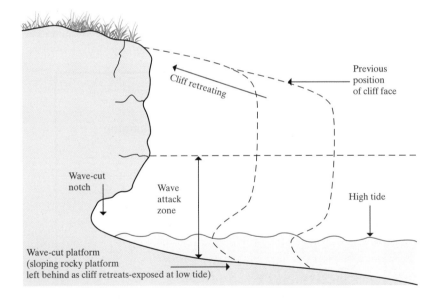

Fig 3
Cliff erosion and wave-cut platforms

Examiners' notes

Know your case studies and examples:

- South Stack on Anglesey; nearby Trearddur Bay reveals a wave-cut platform at low tide.
- The south coast of Iceland near Vik has a natural arch called Dyrhólaey.
- On the Dorset coast: Old Harry is a stack with his Wife an example of a stump; a line of stacks called the Pinnacles follow the coast towards Swanage; Durlston Head has a wave-cut platform; nearby Durdle Door is an example of an arch.
- Flamborough Head in Yorkshire has caves, arches, stacks, blow holes and a wave-cut platform.

Landforms of deposition

A beach has different zones caused by wave action:

- **Ridges and runnels** caused by strong backwash run parallel to the shore line.
- The **storm beach** is developed through strong swash during spring tides and storms, with the largest-sized beach material found here.
- **Berms** mark the position of lower tides after the spring tide, often in the form of a small ridge and accumulation of seaweed.
- **Beach cusps** develop where beaches are made of sand and shingle. The sand is worn away more easily than the shingle and creates a semicircular hollow like a miniature bay formation.
- **Ripples** are small beach ridges parallel to the shoreline created by wave action, and are found in the inter-tidal zone.

Spits are long, narrow stretches of sand or shingle which stick out into the sea. They result from materials being moved along the shore by longshore drift. This movement continues along the coast in the same direction. If the coastline curves inward the material continues to be deposited in a forward direction sticking out from the shoreline until a strong current, usually from a river estuary, interrupts the movement of material and carries it away. The end of the spit is often curved where waves are refracted around the end into the more sheltered water behind. This is also helped by the direction of the second most dominant wind. If a spit joins the mainland at one end to an island at the other it is called a **tombolo**.

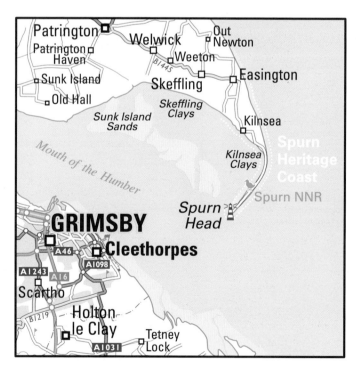

Fig 4
Spurn Head

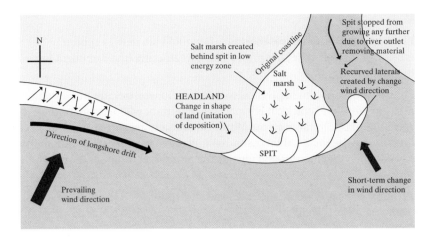

Fig 5
The formation of a spit

Examiners' notes

Good examples of features formed by deposition include the following:

- Spits at Spurn Head at the mouth of the Humber (**fig 4**), and Hurst Castle Spit, Hampshire.
- Chesil beach, which joins the mainland of Dorset near Burton Bradstock to the Isle of Portland (Portland Bill) via a 30-km long shingle ridge, is a tombolo.
- An example of a bar is at Slapton in Devon with a freshwater lagoon called Slapton Ley formed behind it.

Bars: occur where a spit has developed right across a bay because there are no strong currents to disturb the process, water is dammed behind it forming a lagoon. Bars also develop as a result of storms raking up pebbles and shingle left in ridges offshore at the end of the last ice age.

Sand dunes: these consist of mounds of sand blown from the beach inland by onshore winds. Wet sand will stabilize, especially if there is some obstacle such as seaweed or vegetation to anchor it. Embryo dunes develop first with couch grass holding it together. In the foredunes marram grass takes over, as this is well adapted to these conditions. It has rhizomes to help it spread underground, thin leaves to reduce transpiration, and long roots to pick up any moisture. The grey dunes further inland retain more moisture; fescue and other grasses dominate. A dune slack may be reached where the sand has been blown out revealing the water table. Juncus and other marsh-loving plants develop here.

Salt marshes: where silt and mud collects and is not washed away by strong tides or currents, vegetation which tolerates salty wet conditions will grow. Eelgrass and spartina grass, which have a long root system and a mat of surface roots, hold the silt in place. These plants trap more mud and build up a soil for the next stage, encouraging plants such as sea lavender.

Fig 6
Iceland beach bar near Vik

Essential notes

There is controversy about protection of the Slapton bar as it has been breached by storms on many occasions. One suggestion will allow the bar to be breached which will turn the freshwater ley into a salt marsh. The road to the village would be cut isolating this area further. For further information, visit: www.slaptonline.org

Weathering

Land-based sub-aerial weathering: when rocks are newly exposed by erosion at the coast they are prone to fast weathering (the disintegration of the rock *in situ*).

Freeze-thaw is a form of physical weathering, in which water freezes and melts in joints and cracks; it is especially important where temperatures stay around 0°C for a long time. Water expands on freezing and exerts pressure on the rock. It then melts, refilling the now larger crack with more water, which then freezes and repeats the process, causing shattering of the rock.

Pressure release is where the rock is newly exposed and the pressure of overlying rocks is suddenly released, causing the rock to crack. Salt crystal growth also cracks rocks open.

Biological weathering comes from organic sources. These can be plant roots or animal burrows, which can weather exposed rocks in the inter-tidal zone. There is a shellfish called a piddock which bores into rock leaving small depressions in a flat rock surface.

Chemical weathering is caused by a range of chemical processes:

- **Oxidation**, where iron in rocks is exposed to air and oxidizes into ferric oxide (rust) which breaks up and crumbles.
- **Hydrolysis**, where the hydrogen and hydroxide ions in water combine with mineral ions and cause breakdown of minerals.
- **Hydration**, where some rocks contain mineral salts which absorb water and swell, causing decomposition.
- **Carbonation**, where rainwater absorbs carbon dioxide from the atmosphere to form a weak solution of carbonic acid. This weathers limestone, speeding up erosion by solution.

Mass movement

Weathered rocks exposed at the coast are unstable, and mass movements are common. These include:

- **Rock falls** – large rocks fall rapidly and suddenly, usually as a result of undercutting by marine erosion.
- **Landslides** – slides keep their internal structure whilst moving down slope, and move as a large mass.
- **Rotational slumping** - where rock structure is weak, particularly in clays. Rotational slumping occurs after heavy rainfall and the raising of the water table; this reduces the internal friction of particles, causing the slope to fail. The front section flows, producing a lobe at the base of the slope.

Essential notes

Atmospheric gases from burning of fossil fuels, including sulphur dioxide, nitrous oxides as well as carbon dioxide accelerate this process by the production of even more acidic rain.

Case study of coastal erosion: Flamborough Head and Holderness

Physical causes of erosion: At Flamborough Head the chalk rock has many joints and bedding planes which are easily eroded by wave action to form caves, arches and stacks on the headland. Although it is a harder rock than the boulder clay further south it is gradually being eroded by the waves. Storms from the northeast provide the most powerful wave action and tides carry material southwards. When beaches are undermined by waves, revealing the boulder clay beneath the sand, the beach no longer protects the cliffs behind and erosion occurs.

Human causes: There is a concern that the recent dredging of aggregates offshore may have affected sediment flows in the area and led to more erosion. Building on the cliff tops has increased runoff and may have made the cliffs more unstable. Coastal defences built to protect the cliff line in the past can actually cause more erosion locally as it concentrates the power of the waves at the next undefended section.

Fig 7
The Holderness coast near Aldborough, which is being actively eroded

Physical effects: Since Roman times over 30 villages have been lost to the sea; the Holderness area just south of Flamborough Head is eroding fast, at about 1.5 m per year.

Social and economic consequences: This coast is strewn with the remains of forts, houses, roads and drains which are still falling into the sea. People have lost their homes and livelihood and others cannot get a mortgage or insurance for housing here. The natural gas terminal at Easington is under threat; roads and communications are being cut and farmland has been lost, including a dairy farm. People cannot afford to repair or even demolish damaged property and only caravan sites now exist along much of the coast.

Essential notes

If sea walls are too straight they can increase wave power. This has a knock-on effect increasing erosion further along the coast.

Essential notes

Large rocks can be used but they are often removed by powerful waves and used as ammunition to batter the coast, so rip-rap is more useful.

Essential notes

Human activity at the coast can increase erosion, for example by footpath erosion, the weight of buildings causing stress on weak cliffs, or trampling through sand dunes and causing blow outs.

Essential notes

Some schemes use a variety of different techniques in a short section of coast. For example, in Pevensey Bay, East Sussex, between Eastbourne and Bexhill, authorities have used:

- Beach replenishment using materials from the Hastings banks;
- Beach re-proofing moving materials back along the beach after the winter storms;
- A retaining wall made of wood and steel and rubble buried in the shingle to keep the pebbles in place;
- Some hard engineering, such as groynes, to prevent material moving along the shoreline.

Coastal management

There are several ways of providing coastal protection, the most expensive being **hard engineering**. This is where sea protection is built out of concrete or rocks providing permanent defences. Defence types include:

- **Sea wall** – made of stone or concrete to withstand the force of the waves, often curved to reflect waves and reduce their power;
- **Revetment** – sloping concrete wall or wooden slats;
- **Gabions** – wire cages filled with rocks;
- **Groynes** – fences or low walls to prevent longshore drift;
- **Rip-rap (rock armour)** – boulders of various shapes which often lock together to break up the waves;
- **Offshore breakwater (whale back)** – protects the shore line from the waves and can build up protective sediment;
- **Barriers/dams/barrages** – built to control river estuaries.

Soft engineering uses natural materials and processes to help to protect coastline, including:

- **Beach replenishment** – adding more beach materials to keep a beach in place;
- Use of **sand dunes** (sometimes artificially protected from further erosion) to act as a natural barrier;
- **Marsh creation** – providing an area for the sea to enter to relieve the pressure of waves on the rest of the coast;
- **Land use and activity management** – planning regulations to limit building at the coast and tourism management, such as board walks
- **Managed retreat** – allowing some areas of the coastline to be breached. These areas absorb wave energy, and allow any sediment produced to be moved by the waves along the shoreline and naturally protect other areas. Such strategies are cheap to implement and often create new wetlands. Farmland is lost and communications are often cut, so there is compensation and a relocation cost involved, and so this would not be suitable in densely populated areas e.g. the Blackwater Estuary, Essex.
- **Do nothing** is often a positive option.

Cost benefit analysis

Where coastal erosion or flooding is a problem, decisions about coastal management have to weigh up the advantages and disadvantages of each option and consider the cost implications. This is called cost benefit analysis. In areas where there is a high population density, expensive coastal protection schemes using hard engineering are the usual option. However, this can cause problems elsewhere along the coast and it is not practicable to build sea defences around the whole coast of Britain. For example, in Lyme Regis the total cost was £33 million to protect the main part of the town. It took into account the number of properties it would protect for which no compensation would then need to be paid. It also included the improved appearance and use of the seafront areas and public gardens, with a predicted increase in tourist income. The local authorities did not extend the scheme to the east because this is part of the heritage coast and no sea defences would be allowed here. The active erosion of the cliffs towards Charmouth was not protected as it was thought that any sediment produced from this would help to build up beaches further along the coast, which would help to protect these places.

Any scheme has to show that the potential benefits (given a monetary value) outweigh the costs of implementing the scheme.

Sustainable management has to work with natural processes. Soft engineering is more sustainable than hard engineering. In some cases where land is of low economic value it has been decided to do nothing: to allow erosion and pay any resulting compensation. This is often a cheaper option and may help to protect other areas of coast, but is not popular amongst the local people. It can create new marshlands which have environmental advantages and are sustainable. Other options are **managed realignment**, which allows for a retreat of current sea defences. Managed realignment has been used on the Blackwater estuary in Essex, at Abbots Hall Farm: the original sea walls were allowed to be breached and a new line of defences was built further inland. This has saved £500,000 by not rebuilding the sea defences.

Holding the line involves building higher defences and **advancing the line** means building new flood defences seawards. These last two options are less sustainable, especially if sea levels rise.

Case studies: coastal protection

Hard engineering: North Wales coast – From Prestatyn to Llandudno the Welsh coast is prone to erosion and flooding. Coastal defences have been built in the area around Llanddulas to prevent erosion of limestone cliffs, damage to the main A55 road and railway line, and to protect a quay for unloading limestone from the quarry. Concrete tetra pods acting as also protect the pebble beach at Llanddulas, with revetments and gabions protecting key points. There is a sea wall at Colwyn Bay and further east, at Rhos on Sea, is an offshore breakwater (whaleback) which encourages the deposition of sand to protect the harbour and sea wall. There are groynes along much of the coastline to prevent longshore drift of beach material, and each year the local council digs the sand back to make the beach more level, often replenishing it as well. At Llandudno a sea wall and revetments help to reduce the effect of the waves.

Soft engineering: Netherlands dunes (north of the Hague) – The west coast of Holland consists of a large area of continuous sand dunes which are being washed away by the sea each year. As the sand is washed out to sea the beaches are lowered and the dunes behind are prone to wave attack. Sand mixed with water is collected from the deep sea bed about 20km off shore. This is then sprayed onto the beach to aid the protection provided by the beach by sand replenishment. Grasses and trees are planted so that their roots help to stabilise the beach. Some areas of the dunes are fenced off to stop people eroding the dunes.

Essential notes

In Bangladesh, where coastal flooding is a regular and large-scale occurrence, the country cannot afford to implement expensive hard engineering projects. Some embankments have been raised and sluice gates installed to help to manage the issue. Mangrove trees have also been planted to encourage the growth of mangrove swamps which act as a buffer zone. Other actions involve mitigating the effects by improving warning systems and building flood shelters on stilts or on higher land.

Essential notes

The Conwy County Borough council website has information about the coastal management of north Wales: www.conwy.gov.uk

Examiners' notes

Choose examples of coastal management schemes which illustrate a variety of different ideas or points of view when answering exam questions.

Sea level change and coastal flooding

Sea level changes over time due to sea temperatures changing or relative changes in land levels.

Eustatic change refers to changes which affect worldwide sea levels. They may result from a fall in sea level due to a new glacial period, when water is held as ice. At the end of glaciation the ice on land melts and global sea levels rise again.

Isostatic change refers to local changes in land and sea levels. During glaciation, as ice collects on the land the extra weight presses down on the land causing it to sink, and sea level to rise. As the land ice melts the land begins to move back up to its original position (isostatic readjustment), and sea level falls. This process is variable, depending on the thickness of the original ice and the speed of its melting. If land rises faster than sea level rises, emergent features develop. Land also rises and falls relative to sea level due to tectonic movement.

Coastlines of submergence

Rias: these are drowned river valleys (including tributary valleys) with long fingers of water stretching a long way inland, e.g. Carrick Roads, Falmouth, where the river Fal and its tributaries have been drowned by rising sea levels to form a wide and deep natural harbour.

Fjords: these are glaciated valleys near the coast which have been drowned by the rising sea level at the end of the ice age. They often have a shallower area at the mouth called a threshold where the ice thinned as it reached the sea; e.g. Hardanger fjord in Norway.

Coastlines of emergence

Raised beaches: as the coastline rises (or sea level falls) beaches which were once at sea level are left high up in the cliffs, e.g. on the Isle of Arran.

Relict cliffs: in some areas, features of erosion are found above the shoreline. Caves, arches and stacks formed when they were at sea level are now left high up on a cliff face above the present-day coastal features. This is evident along the Amalfi coast in Italy, where tectonic processes have caused uplift of the coastline.

Impact of sea level increase

As Britain recovers from the last ice age, the north and west of Britain, which was covered by ice, is springing back and land levels are rising. Further east and southeast, land subsidence has resulted in loss of coastline and sometimes whole villages. Areas most at risk from present-day flooding are London and the lower Thames, the Fens and the Humber estuary. This, combined with the fast erosion of the cliffs in areas such as Holderness, puts human activities in danger. Sea level increase has implications for groundwater supply, which may become contaminated with salt water creep, and could cause flooding of salt marshes and loss of habitats. Insurance premiums on any developments in these areas will also rise.

Examiners' notes

You may need to refer to:

- Physical effects – the areas flooded and the damage to landscape
- Social and economic effects – affecting jobs, finance and lifestyle
- Environmental effects – affecting habitats and wildlife.

Coastal flooding

This can be caused by a number of factors: storm surges, tropical cyclones, tsunamis and global warming. If global temperatures continue to rise and land ice melts, global sea levels will rise. Warmer sea temperatures also cause sea levels to rise, as warm water expands. Worldwide, many low-lying areas are at risk of flooding, e.g. the Maldives and Bangladesh.

Case study: the Lower Thames basin and the Thames Barrier

Causes: London is subsiding geologically and the surface is sinking due to the drying out of clay. Sea levels are rising due to global warming. The funnel shape of the Thames estuary makes it vulnerable to storm surges. On 1 February 1953 low pressure tracked down the North Sea which allowed sea level to rise by 0.5 m. High spring tides and strong northerly winds produced waves over 6 m high approaching the narrowing southern part of the North Sea. This pushed a wall of water into the Thames estuary.

Effects: The waves broke through sea defences and caused coastal flooding over a wide area. Over 250 people drowned along the whole of the east coast, salt marsh habitats were destroyed, and buildings, communications and farmland were damaged.

The Thames Barrier was built in 1982 to help stop the river flooding London. The barrier is a series of 10 separate movable gates across the river. Closing the barrier closes off part of the river from the sea. When not in use, the gates rest in the riverbed, which allows river traffic to pass through.

Figures from the Environment Agency show that over the last 25 years the Thames Barrier has closed 106 times, over half of which closures have occurred since 2000. Without this barrier it is possible that London itself would flood, affecting important buildings such as the Houses of Parliament and the government offices on Whitehall. Such a flood, as well as endangering life, would force the London Underground to close and cause damage to the built environment amounting to billions of pounds. It is thought that the barrier will not be able to cope after 2030, and there are plans to build extra defences and even another barrier.

Locations and characteristics of hot desert environments and their margins

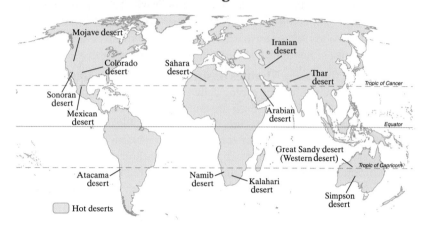

Fig 1
Location of major hot desert areas

The hot deserts can be classified as being **arid** (< 250 mm precipitation per year) and **semi-arid** (250 mm to 500 mm precipitation per year).

Hot desert temperatures are characterised by their extremes. These occur both:

- **Diurnally** (between day and night) – the clear skies allow both intense insolation during the day and rapid heat loss to space at night. Diurnal ranges of 15–20 °C are common.
- **Annually** (throughout the year) – latitude is the most important factor in the annual range; the further away from the tropics the desert is, the greater the range.

Semi-arid areas vary greatly in their temperature patterns. Those on the equatorial side of the deserts are much hotter than those on the poleward sides.

Plants in hot deserts are mainly low woody shrubs and trees. Leaves are 'replete' (fully supported with nutrients) and water-conserving; they tend to be small, thick, and covered with a thick cuticle (outer layer). In cacti, the leaves are reduced to spines and photosynthesis is restricted to the stems. Some plants open their stomata (microscopic openings in the epidermis of leaves that allow for gas exchange) only at night, when evaporation rates are lowest. These plants include: yuccas, ocotillo and prickly pears.

The large numbers of spines on plants in semi-arid areas shade the surface enough to significantly reduce transpiration. The same is true of the hairs on the woolly desert plants. Many plants have silvery or glossy leaves, allowing them to reflect more insolation. Semi-arid plants include the creosote bush and jujube.

Soils in hot deserts are coarse-textured, shallow, rocky or gravely with little organic matter. This is caused by low plant productivity, which restricts the soil-building properties of microorganisms. Soils with low organic matter content have a low water-holding capacity. This, added to the intense evaporation of water from desert soils, tends to bring dissolved salts to the surface. The high surface content of sodium and calcium ions can lead to extensive saltpans. The soils of semi-arid areas are dependent on their location. They can range from sandy and fine-textured to loose rock fragments, gravel or sand.

Essential notes

The typical soil of hot deserts is called an **aridisol**, and the soil of semi-arid areas is called a solonetz. The characteristics of soils can be shown by a soil profile. Draw a profile of each of the above named soils.

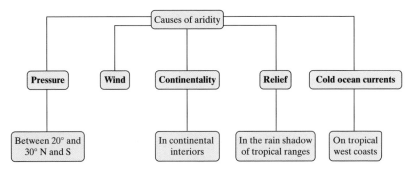

Fig 2
The five main causes of aridity

Continentality: The further an area is from the influence of the sea and the moist air that flows off it, the drier it is. Some parts of the Sahara desert are almost 2000 km from the sea.

Relief: Land downwind of mountains is said to be in a **rain shadow**. Air rises over the mountains and cools, forming relief rain on the upwind side. When the air subsequently descends it has not only lost some of the moisture content, but it also warms on descent, giving cloudless skies, e.g. the Atacama desert.

Cold ocean currents: There are four major cold currents that flow along the western shores of tropical regions. Any air blowing from the ocean over the current is cooled by it. This condenses into fog. This fog can be blown onshore, but is quickly evaporated during the day. Also, the cool air is not able to hold very much water vapour and as it passes onto the land it is warmed, so that the air becomes very dry, e.g. the Namib desert.

Pressure and winds: In sub-tropical regions (25˚–35˚ N and S), high atmospheric pressure dominates. The high pressure is the result of falling air. This descending air is compressed and warms, evaporating any water droplets. This leaves the sky clear of cloud. This, coupled with the high angle of the sun, gives dry hot climates, e.g. the Sahara desert.

Examiners' notes

Well-drawn and annotated diagrams can add much to an answer. Create three easy-to-reproduce annotated diagrams to explain the influence of pressure, rain shadow and ocean currents on causing aridity. Include one example of a desert area for each.

Arid geomorphological processes

Mechanical weathering takes place in hot deserts because of the high diurnal range in temperatures. The range in surface temperatures of rocks can be as much as 75 °C and can lead to four main processes:

- **Granular disintegration** occurs in rocks that comprise minerals of different colours. Darker minerals absorb more heat than lighter ones (e.g. black mica expands more than grey quartz) and so the rock breaks up grain by grain to produce sand-sized material.
- **Exfoliation** (onion skin weathering) is most noticeable on rocks with few joints or bedding planes (e.g. granite, massive sandstone). It occurs because the surface heat does not penetrate very deeply into these rocks. The outer layers expand and contract daily, but the interior does not. This differential leads to weaknesses parallel to the surface. Layers peel off the rock.
- **Block separation** occurs predominantly on well-jointed and bedded limestones, where the rock breaks up into blocks along these weaknesses.
- Rocks that are microcrystalline are subject to **shattering** by constant diurnal expansion and contraction, e.g. basalt. **Frost shattering** can occur in deserts where there is some free water and the night-time temperatures fall below zero. The water gets into fractures in the rock, freezes at night and so expands. Continual freezing and thawing will result in fragments breaking off.

The effects of wind

Wind is able to erode desert surfaces. It does this in two ways:

- **Deflation**: loose, fine material is picked up by the wind and is transported and deposited elsewhere. It can create depressions in the desert floor (**deflation hollows**), e.g. the Qattara depression in Egypt. It can also remove fine sand from a surface, leaving behind coarser stones that blanket the surface to form a reg or **desert pavement** (fig 4).
- **Abrasion** (the sand-blasting effect): fine material carried in the wind is blown at rocks. This has a polishing effect. The rocks which are struck by the sand grains form landforms such as yardangs and zeugens (see p 46). The coarsest material, which has the greatest effect, cannot be lifted more than 1.5 m off the ground. This results in undercutting.

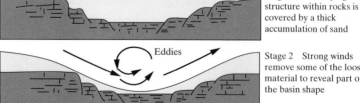

Stage 1   Underlying basin structure within rocks is covered by a thick accumulation of sand

Stage 2   Strong winds remove some of the loose material to reveal part of the basin shape

Fig 3
The creation of deflation hollows

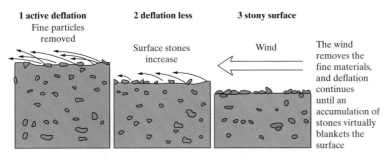

1 active deflation
Fine particles removed

2 deflation less
Surface stones increase

3 stony surface
Wind

The wind removes the fine materials, and deflation continues until an accumulation of stones virtually blankets the surface

Fig 4
The creation of desert pavements through deflation

Wind is able to **transport** material in three ways:

- **Saltation**: the coarser grains of sand move in a series of hops across the surface. A grain is picked up, carried a short distance, and then dropped by the wind. Where it falls it can dislodge other grains that are then picked up.
- **Suspension**: high velocity winds can lift and carry fine silt and clay high into the atmosphere. This can often be taken away from the desert area entirely.
- **Surface creep**: coarse grains of sand are rolled across the surface.

Water in deserts
Sources of water in the desert include:

- Large perennial rivers that originate outside the desert are called **exogeneous rivers.** The River Nile's main tributary, the Blue Nile, originates in the Ethiopian Highlands. These have a monsoon climate, with a four-month wet season. This continually feeds the river, though the amount varies through the year.
- There are perennial rivers that flow into an inland drainage basin in the desert; e.g. the river Jordan flows into the Dead Sea which, at 422 m below sea level, has no outlet. These are called **endoreic rivers**.
- When there is a heavy rainstorm in a desert, the rain cannot infiltrate the baked desert surface. Water flows over land as sheet flow in what are normally dry valleys (**wadis**). After the storm the water quickly evaporates or soaks into the wadi floor. These rivers are called **ephemeral rivers**.

The role of flooding
Flooding, although rare, does occur in deserts. In October 2003, for example, the southern part of the desert territory of Western Sahara experienced the heaviest rains in several years, causing wadis and temporary lakes to be created. These temporary floods are crucial for the fragile ecosystem of the desert area as they fill up groundwater basins that provide water in the more normal periods of water shortage.

Examiners' notes

You must make it clear in your answers that the sand is picked up and carried by the wind so that it can be thrown against rocks to erode them.

Examiners' notes

It is useful to have a case study of each type of water source. This enables the examiner to see that the differences between them are understood.

Desert landforms

Landforms resulting from wind action

Zeugens form where there are large areas of horizontal rock layers with vertical jointing. The weak joints are eroded by abrasion and then softer layers are eroded underneath. Thus, long ridges develop with a protective cap rock.

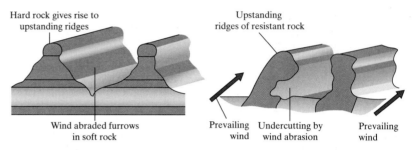

Fig 5
Zeugen (left) and yardangs (right)

Yardangs occur when the layers of rock lie at a steep angle to the surface and parallel to the prevailing wind. The less resistant rock layers are eroded more rapidly than the resistant ones, leaving long ridges. These can be several kilometres long and hundreds of metres high.

Landforms resulting from deposition

Sand dunes are formed by the reworking, by the wind, of large deposits of sand. Loose sand is blown up the windward side of a dune. The sand particles then fall to rest on the downwind side, while more are blown up from the windward side. In this way a dune moves gradually downwind. In sandy deserts, the typical crescent-shaped dune is called a barchan. Seif dunes are longitudinal and lie parallel to the wind direction. Seif dunes can be very long (>100km) and can reach 200m in height. Star-shaped dunes are formed where no one wind direction is dominant. Where these coalesce into a serrated ridge, a draa dune is formed, which can be up to 400m high and tens of kilometres long.

Water action in deserts

Most of the large-scale landforms in a desert are the result of water. They then have been further shaped by wind and weather. Landforms created by water erosion include the following:

- **Inselbergs**: This is a generic term for any relic hills found in deserts. They were probably formed by deep chemical weathering of crystalline rock when the climate was wetter. They have subsequently been exposed by water removing the surface deposits.
- **Mesas and buttes**: These are particular forms of inselbergs. They are formed in areas of sedimentary rocks with horizontal bedding planes. Water has eroded the land around them, leaving some resistant portions, with a resistant cap rock standing out from the surface. Mesas are steep-sided and flat-topped. Buttes are similar, but are much more eroded and are pillar-like in appearance. Their lower slopes are often covered in scree, the result of weathering.

Fig 6
Mesas and buttes in Monument
Valley, Utah, USA

- **Pediments** are extensive, low-angled (1–7°) rock surfaces at the base of desert mountain ranges. Their origin is uncertain, but it is thought that they may have been formed by the retreat of the mountain front by weathering accompanied by **sheet erosion**. This is the removal of thin layers of surface material evenly from an extensive area of gently sloping land by broad continuous sheets of running water.
- **Wadis** are dry valleys found in deserts. They are formed either by ephemeral or endoreic rivers. When the rivers are flowing, they carry huge amounts of sediment. They are able to erode vertically (aided by the lack of vegetation) to form the steep sides. When the rivers dry up, this sediment is deposited on the floor of the wadi, to give a flat floor.
- **Badlands topography** occurs where softer sedimentary rocks and clay-rich soils have been extensively eroded by water and wind. Canyons, ravines, gullies, hoodoos and other such geological forms are common in badlands.

Depositional landforms

Deposition occurs when the wind can no longer move the desert material. These deposits can then be shaped by the wind.

Alluvial fans occur where rivers in wadis emerge from upland areas. As soon as the river leaves the confines of the wadi, it spreads out and deposits the sediment. Where several wadis emerge, the alluvial fans coalesce and form a bajada.This may cover up the pediment.

Salt lakes are formed where there is an inland drainage basin. Ephemeral and endoreic streams flow to the lowest point in the desert. There the high temperatures cause the river water to evaporate, leaving the dissolved salts behind. In Death Valley, California, sodium borate (borax) is extracted for industrial use.

Essential notes

The most common dissolved salts left behind in salt lakes are sodium chloride (common salt) and calcium sulphate (gypsum).

Desertification

The United Nations Convention to Combat Desertification (UNCCD) defines desertification as 'land degradation in arid, semi-arid and dry sub-humid areas resulting from various factors, including climatic variations and human activities. Land degradation is in turn defined as 'the reduction or loss of the biological or economic productivity of drylands'.

Examiners' notes

Learn how to describe a global distribution from a world map such as this. Use reference points such as: tropical, equatorial, northern hemisphere, north Africa etc. Note: naming individual countries does not give a clear description of distribution.

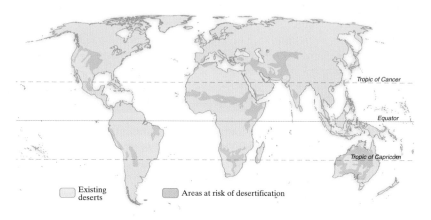

Fig 7
Areas at risk from desertification

Existing deserts   Areas at risk of desertification

Examiners' notes

The causes of climate change are irrelevant when discussing desertification in the examination.

The main causes of **desertification** can be divided into physical and human causes.

The main physical cause is climate change. In the vulnerable areas the following changes are taking place:

- There is less rainfall, and what there is, is less reliable. This means farmers find it difficult to plan ahead. There is an increase in drought frequency and intensity.
- There are higher temperatures. This increases evaporation, reduces condensation and leads to less rainfall.
- Because there is less rainfall, rivers dry up and the water table falls.

The main human cause is population growth. The number of people is increasing in some of the at-risk areas because of high birth rates and an influx of refugees from conflict or drought-hit areas. Population growth may lead to:

- Increasing livestock numbers. This leads to **overgrazing**.
- Change from a nomadic to a more sedentary type of agriculture because of lack of land and the need to grow more food crops.
- The increasing demand for **fuel wood**, which leads to deforestation.

The changing nature of world trade in food has led to:

- An increase in the growing of cash crops for markets in the more developed world (e.g. coffee in Ethiopia). This means that the best land is used for these crops and unsuitable marginal land is used for growing food crops.

The decreasing amount of rainfall and the changing land use has seen an increase in unsuitable irrigation practices. These lead to salinization.

All of these factors lead to destruction of the vegetation cover. Soil is then exposed to the wind and rain, which in turn leads to **soil erosion** because the root mat that holds the soil together is gone. This loss of soil then leads to desertification.

Case study of desertification in the Sahel

The Sahel region is found in sub-Saharan Africa, and constitutes a semi-arid strip of land across the full width of the continent. The Sahel is a transition zone between the arid north and the tropical forest to the south, covering a surface area of 5.4 million km^2 with a population of about 50 million inhabitants. The vegetation in the Sahel region is composed of mainly stunted and scattered trees, shrubs, bushes and grasses.

In the **struggle for survival** the people of the Sahel have to overcome:

- **The climate**: The Sahel has a seasonal wet season/dry season climate. The wet season occurs between June and September. The rainfall totals are low, with frequent droughts. Agadez in the Sahel region of Niger receives 165 mm per year. Rainfall occurs in short, intense thunderstorms. There is drought for the rest of the year. The temperatures are high, averaging between 31 °C and 41 °C. In November, a hot dry wind (the Harmattan) blows from the Sahara desert.
- **Population growth** is high. In Niger it is estimated to be growing by 3.9% per year and that the rate of increase is growing. It has the highest birth rate in the world with 51.6 per thousand.
- **Deforestation**: The Sahel has no developed fossil fuel resources. People rely on wood for cooking. This, along with clearance of land for agriculture, has led to removal of the native forest. Niger lost 34.9% of its forest cover, around 679 000 hectares, between 1990 and 2005.
- **Water supply**: There is a lack of water in the Sahel. This is not only because of the lack of rainfall, but an inability to access deep groundwater sources. Niger has an estimated 2.5 bn m^3 of underground renewable water, but only 20% is currently exploited. Only 60% of Niger's rural population has access to safe drinking water.

All of the above factors have led to the soil being depleted. The exposed soil is washed away by the rainstorms, or blown away by strong dry winds. The growing population needs more food crops and so forest is cleared. This exposes the soil to erosion. This has led to a deterioration of the food and livestock situation. In Niger, 7.1 million people – 48% of the population are – estimated to be food insecure, including 3.3 million people facing 'severe' **food insecurity**.

Examiners' notes

Questions about this part of the specification will focus on why it is a struggle to survive here, and what people have done about it.

Examiners' notes

The specification states that you must have a case study of desertification in the Sahel. Add to the information opposite by researching:

- The traditional farming systems of a named area
- Developments by farmers, at a local level, to cope with drought, e.g. community schemes to purchase food in Niger
- The role of external aid agencies, e.g. Oxfam in Niger.

Managing hot desert environments and their margins

The southwest USA is probably the most economically developed desert area in the world. This study will concentrate on the state of Nevada.

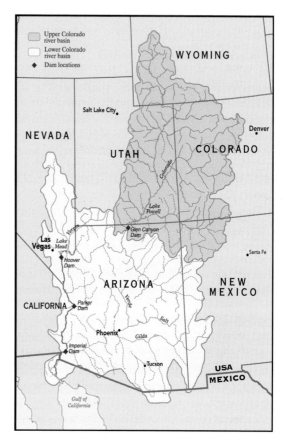

Fig 8
Map of the Colorado river basin

The climate statistics for Las Vegas show that it is located in a true desert. The total annual rainfall is 114 mm and the summer temperatures are very high.

Month	Jan	Feb	Mar	Apr	May	Jun	Jul	Aug	Sept	Oct	Nov	Dec
Average day temperature °C	14	17	21	26	31	37	40	39	34	27	19	14
Average night temperature °C	3	5	8	12	17	22	26	25	20	14	7	3
Precipitation (mm)	15	17.5	15	3.8	6.1	2	11.2	11.4	7.9	6.1	7.9	10.2
Average days with rain	3.4	3.5	3.6	1.8	1.6	0.7	2.6	3.0	1.9	1.8	1.8	2.9
Sunshine hours	244.9	248.6	313.1	345.0	387.5	402.0	390.6	368.9	336.0	303.8	246.0	235.6

Table 1
Climate statistics for Las Vegas, Nevada

Climate change: By 2100, the average temperatures for Nevada are expected to increase by 2°C in the spring and autumn and by 2°C in the summer and winter. Increasing temperatures will affect the rate of water evaporation and precipitation in the state. Nevada is expected to have wetter winters and more arid summers. Higher temperatures and increased winter rainfall will be accompanied by a reduction in snow, earlier snowmelts, and increased runoff.

Water supply: The main source of water for this area is the exogeneous Colorado river. It runs 2 300 km through five states, eventually flowing through Mexico to the Gulf of California. Its source is high in the Rocky Mountains of Colorado where it is fed by snow meltwater. Water is stored in a series of reservoirs along the Colorado river. Lake Mead is the main source of water for Las Vegas. From 1999 to 2009, following the worst 10-year drought in recorded history along the Colorado river, Lake Mead dropped about 1% a year. As of October 2007, Lake Mead stood at only 49% capacity.

Population growth: The population of the city of Las Vegas grew by 14% between 2000 and 2005. This growth was fed by the in-migration of many retirees. Older people see the dry climate and the all-year-round sunshine as very attractive.

Agriculture: The main agriculture of Nevada is livestock rearing. This is done on large ranches. Ranchers have suffered from the lack of water during the latest drought. Irrigation accounted for about 83% of total groundwater withdrawals in Nevada. Irrigated crops grown in Nevada include alfalfa and other hay, winter and spring wheat, potatoes, alfalfa seed, and vegetables. Harvested croplands account for approximately 70% of all irrigated lands, with the remaining 30% being irrigated pasture. There is increasing conflict between the farmers and urban areas over dwindling water resources.

Impacts of water shortage: Some 2 million people in Las Vegas alone depend on Lake Mead for daily water needs and the Hoover Dam provides energy to roughly 1.3 million people in Nevada, Arizona, and California. The changes to Lake Mead have presented challenges in order to satisfy the rising demand for water from Las Vegas. One study suggests that unless water consumption is drastically reduced, Lake Mead will dry up by 2021, leaving 12–36 million people without a secure water supply. Lake Mead also generates $1bn annually from tourism and recreation.

Sustainability: It is clear that Nevada cannot continue as it is. Water resources are rapidly disappearing. Rather than the city of Las Vegas reducing its water consumption, it has applied for water rights to huge tracts of ranch land in the north of the state and for permission to build a 480 km pipeline to transport the water.

Examiners' notes

Draw a table to make direct comparisons between each aspect of the two case studies, the Sahel and Nevada. Use this in preparation for an extended essay on this topic.

Examiners' notes

Population change is the core Human section and all candidates must study this section.

Examiners' notes

While you won't be expected to remember a long list of statistics, a few key ones do provide evidence for your answers. Always make sure you refer to any statistics provided in tables and graphs when you answer exam questions.

Essential notes

For up-to-date statistics on aspects of population, the Population Reference Bureau has data sheets giving figures for recent years, at: www.prb.org/publications/datasheets.aspx

Population indicators

Population is measured by collecting data through counts and censuses. There are a number of key indicator statistics which show how a population is changing and give an idea of the standard of living, level of economic development, and pressure on resources.

Birth rate is the number of live births per thousand people per year. It is known as the **crude birth rate**. Higher birth rates tend to occur in developing countries. The UK birth rate for 2010 is 13/1 000, in Italy it is 10/1 000, and in Niger it is 52/1 000.

Reasons for high/increasing birth and fertility rates	Reasons for low/decreasing birth and fertility rates
• High infant mortality rate • Children needed to work/help • Little access to artificial contraception • Early marriage • Culture and tradition • Status • Religious beliefs • Poor education • Baby boom after a war/recession	• Low infant mortality rate • Later marriage • Women expect to have careers • Good educational standards • Culture and tradition • Expectations of high living standard • Good access to artificial contraception • Good healthcare • Economic recession

Death rate is the number of deaths per thousand people per year. It is known as the crude death rate. Higher rates tend to occur in developing countries. The UK death rate is 9/1 000, in Italy it is 10/1 000 and in Niger it is 17/1 000. The death rate has become lower worldwide due to advancements in healthcare and sanitation, with the highest being 20/1 000 in Zambia, partly due to the high incidence of HIV/AIDS.

Reasons for high/increasing death rate	Reasons for low/decreasing death rate
• Poor sanitation • Contaminated drinking water • Poor nutrition/famine • War/disasters/poor safety standards • Disease (including HIV/AIDS) • Poor access to healthcare • Poor education	• Good sanitation and hygiene • Clean drinking water • Good nutrition • Good education • Good healthcare • Good social care • Health and safety at work

Fertility rate is the number of live births per thousand women aged 15–49 per year. The total fertility rate is the average number of children each woman in a population will have. Population replacement level is 2.1. In developed countries the fertility rate is falling (total fertility is as low as 1.2 in Italy) whereas in developing countries the rate is well above replacement (a total fertility rate of 7.8 per female in Niger in 2010). There is often a correlation with both the infant mortality rate (Niger 108/1 000 compared with Italy 3.6/1 000) and life expectancy (Niger 48, Italy 82).

Infant mortality rate is the number of children under the age of one who die per thousand live births per year. This will affect average life expectancy, and there is a direct correlation with access to healthcare and clean water.

Changes over time in any population are a result of the differences between the birth and death rates, known as the **natural increase rate**.

Actual increase or decrease will also depend on the impact of immigration and emigration.

If a population is increasing quickly we refer to the time it is expected to take for that population to double as its **doubling time**.

Life expectancy is the average age to which a person is expected to live at birth. Longevity refers to the increase in the average age of life expectancy giving rise to larger numbers living to older ages.

Migration refers to people moving to a different location on a permanent basis. Migration can be local, in which case it will not change the overall figures for any country. International migration can be for a variety of reasons. Economic migrants move for work or to improve their social conditions and their migration may be legal or illegal. Refugees are unable (or unwilling) to return to their country of origin for fear of persecution.

Migration rate is a measure of the balance between immigration and emigration. Net migration is immigration minus emigration per 1,000 population per year.

Essential notes

In the UK in 2010 male life expectancy is 77 years and female 82 years whereas in 2005 it was 76 years for men and 81 years for women so it is rising at a rate of one year for every five years at the moment.

Essential notes

The definition of 'immigrant' and current policy towards immigration can affect the reporting of migration rates from year to year for any particular country.

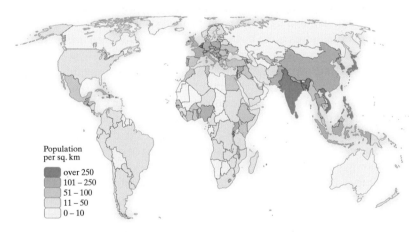

Population per sq. km

- over 250
- 101 – 250
- 51 – 100
- 11 – 50
- 0 – 10

Fig 1
Map of world population density

Population density is the number of people living per unit of land (usually 1 km²). Some countries have a high population density but a high standard of living, e.g. the Netherlands, which has a density of 466.45/km². Others have high density but a lower standard of living, e.g. Bangladesh with 949.38/km². It is more useful as an indicator of pressure on resources.

The Demographic Transition Model (DTM)

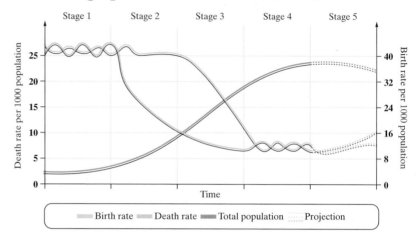

Fig 2
Demographic Transition Model

The model describes the change in the population of a country over time. It is based on the changes in birth and death rates in the UK from before the Industrial Revolution to the end of the 20th century. The original model had four stages; stage 5 has been added later by other authors. The five stages are:

- **Stage 1 (high fluctuating)**: high birth and death rates cancel each other out leading to no or small fluctuating changes in total population, e.g. rainforest tribes.
- **Stage 2 (early expanding)**: birth rate remains high but death rate starts to decrease due to improved hygiene and sanitation. Total population grows rapidly. This is the period in which there is a large difference between the birth and death rate, resulting in a high rate of natural increase, e.g. Kenya,
- **Stage 3 (late expanding)**: the birth rate falls due to lower infant mortality rates, which means more children are likely to survive. Children go to school and are no longer able to work and bring in money for the family. Children are expensive and family planning becomes available so that people can choose the size of their family. The death rate is already low and total population grows more slowly, e.g. Cuba.
- **Stage 4 (low fluctuating)**: birth and death rates are low so the rate of total population growth is very small and fluctuating (birth and death rates again cancel each other out.) Family size is small. Most women work and have careers. A high standard of living is expected, e.g. UK, Canada, Denmark.
- **Stage 5 (decline)**: the death rate is slightly higher than the birth rate so the total population slowly begins to decline. This is possibly due to more women having careers and some deciding not to have children. It may also be a response to concern about the rate of use of resources, e.g. Hungary, Latvia.

The model is very descriptive, and has both advantages and disadvantages.

Advantages:

- It shows change over time, linked to increasing levels of development.
- It can be applied to any country and allows for comparisons to be made.
- It helps to explain what has happened and predict future change for some countries.

Disadvantages:

- It is not as relevant to non-European countries.
- Death rates often fall due to inputs from developed countries, often former colonizers, and therefore have a quick impact.
- Politics, religion and culture impact on the speed of the fall in the birth rate in stage 3, e.g. China's one child policy in the recent past.
- HIV/AIDS in sub-Saharan Africa has increased the death rate in countries which would otherwise be in stage 3.
- Stage 5 had to be added to the original model due to countries in central and eastern Europe having very few children.
- It does not take note of the effect of migration.

In the UK the first four stages took over 200 years to complete but many countries are completing the cycle in just 50 years.

Case study: Iran

Birth rate 2010: 19/1000

Death rate 2010: 6/1000

Population growth rate: 1.3%

This would put Iran at the beginning of stage 3 with a low death rate but a relatively high birth rate which is beginning to decline. Women living in the cities are likely to be more educated, expect to work, marry later and have fewer children. Fertility rate is 2.0 so the population growth will begin to slow. Many Iranians have contacts with people who have migrated and western influences on social and economic attitudes may decrease birth rates further, so Iran could move into stage 4 soon.

Essential notes

Newly industrialised countries (NICs) are going through similar stages but more quickly.

Essential notes

Death rates for some developed countries may appear slightly high because there are more older people in the population at present and hence more deaths.

Population structure

Population structure is the shape of a population by age groups. It is usually shown in a population pyramid. The overall shape suggests which stage of the DTM has been reached:

- **Stage 1**: The more triangular shape shows a wide base indicating a high birth rate and sloping sides to form a peak indicating a steady death rate in all age groups with few elderly.
- **Stage 2**: The sides become slightly more steep showing a decrease in the death rate.
- **Stage 3**: The sides are now steeper but the base is less wide showing a decline in the birth rate.
- **Stage 4**: The shape is like a bell or dome. The sides are steep all the way up to the 65 age group and there is an increase in the height of the pyramid showing more older people.
- **Stage 5**: The base narrows further showing the recent lower birth rate.

The structure of the UK population

Fig 3
Pyramid for the UK 2001 census

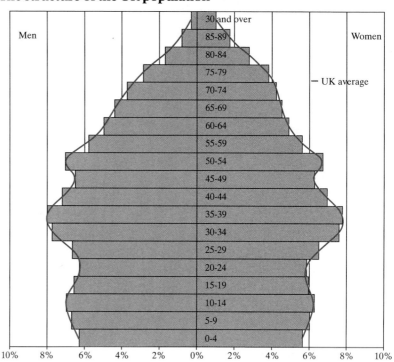

Note the narrow base showing a low birth rate. This has reduced due to social and economic reasons. The lifestyle choices to have holidays, cars and other material possessions made many people delay having families and then often opting for only one child due to women having careers. There is a slightly larger 10–14 age group, possibly reflecting the larger parent age groups of 30–34 and 35–39, which in turn reflects their parent group which is larger (between 50 and 60). These people were born in

Essential notes

There is a census in the UK every 10 years starting in 1841 (apart from 1941 during the war). Visit the UK census website at: www.ons.gov.uk/census/2011

Essential notes

Follow the weblink for www.census.gov/ipc.
Select country, select years, select population pyramid, and use the animation controls at the top of the page to see a population pyramid change for a country. It can predict change for 2025 and 2050. Remember, predicting a future population just requires you to move each age group up the pyramid. You have to estimate future birth rates and cannot account for changes in migration.

the period 1941–1951 (the majority were born in the years immediately after the end of the Second World War in 1945, and are known as 'the baby boomers'). The steep sides show a low death rate in all age groups up to 60+ and after that a steady decline, but still showing a large elderly population. There are more women than men surviving into their 80s and 90s. This is partly due to the effect of the Second World War when male mortality was higher than female, and a society where men often did more dangerous and strenuous jobs such as coal mining.

The **dependency ratio** is an important measure of the economic health of a country. It is the ratio of dependents to workers in a population. It can be calculated by totalling the dependent population (population under 19 plus population over 60) and dividing it by the number of the working population. The higher the ratio the more pressure is put on the working population to support those not working.

Impact of migration on population structure

Migration also affects the shape of a population pyramid.

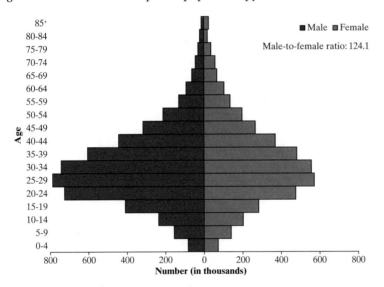

Fig 4
Pyramid for Mexican-born population in the United States, 2000

Out-migration: It is often the young adults (aged 20–34), especially males, who move. This shows as an indent on the male side 20–34. This causes an imbalance in the losing country's population as an ageing population is left behind. This then shows in reduced birth rates and higher death rates, thus exacerbating the loss and causing the decline of services.

In-migration: Again, it is the young adult male population which tends to move into a country or area. This shows as a bulge on the 20–34 male side. As people settle into a new area they tend to have families of their own and the birth rate rises. Often, older people move out of an area and the death rate falls.

This topic continues on the next two pages

Social, economic and political implications of population change

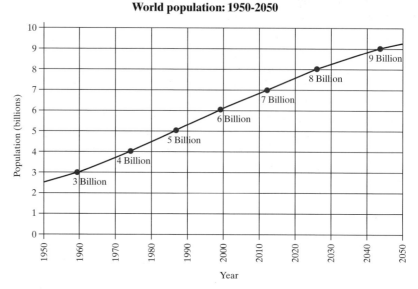

World population: 1950-2050

Fig 5
Recorded and projected world
population growth, 1950–2050

Source: U.S. Census Bureau, International Data Base, June 2010 Update.

On 12 Sept 2010 at 16.20 hrs the world population clock at
http://www.poodwaddle.com/clocks/worldclock/ showed a total
world population of 6,845,532,727 people. Population growth has been
exponential (increasing at an ever-increasing rate) from the Industrial
Revolution until around 1990. The most rapid growth was between 1960
and 2000 but the rate of increase is now slowing down. Total population is
still predicted to increase to 9,485,000,000 by 2050.

Population growth can have negative social and economic effects,
including:

- Increasing unemployment
- Lower standards of living
- Less spending power
- Economic recession and even famine

Population growth can have negative environmental effects, including:

- Overuse of resources
- Desertification
- Extinction of species

Migration effects
Source areas lose the young adults who are often the most skilled and
talented. This may halt investment into the country and cause economic
decline. Social structure is changed as older people and females are left
behind, leaving an imbalance in the population pyramid. In some cases
there are benefits, such as reducing unemployment and pressure on
resources, and new ideas and even cash being sent back to the source
country. Lower population densities may result and income from family

members abroad may increase opportunities for those who remain. Politically, governments may respond with policies to encourage immigration or to encourage births.

Destination areas face increased pressure on services such as health, education and housing. Some industries are over-reliant on migrant labour. Cultural identity can be lost and segregated communities develop, which can lead to discrimination against ethnic groups, civil unrest and demands for immigration controls. There are benefits, however, because economic migrants often take less attractive jobs and/or lower pay. They can fill the gap in skills (e.g. dentists coming from Poland to the UK). A multi-ethnic society is created, with new services and ideas, e.g. the 'curry mile', Rusholme, south Manchester.

Dependency ratios change due to natural increase and decrease or migration. If populations become unbalanced and there are not enough workers to support large numbers of young or older people then the economy may suffer, taxes may have to rise, and services may be put under pressure.

A **young population** has a large number of younger people in proportion to the working population. This puts pressure on education, housing and health services, which support young people and maternity services. It means that there will be a large work force when these youngsters grow up which may help some economies to develop, but other countries may suffer high unemployment rates.

An **ageing population** occurs where there is a large number of older people in proportion to the working population. This puts pressure on the working population to work longer; the pension age may have to rise to provide the increasing numbers of older people with pensions and old-age care. Health service provision will be increasingly stretched as the population gets older, and taxes may rise to provide the services required.

Essential notes

Strategies to limit migration have included:

- Limiting the number of visas available to migrant workers;
- Asking for production of a return ticket at the starting point of a journey;
- Preventing illegal crossings by increasing border patrols (as along the border between Mexico and the USA);
- Building complexes known as 'holding centres'.

Fig 6
'Curry mile', Rusholme, Manchester

Essential notes

The economic effects of ageing populations include changing housing structures, with more purpose-built bungalows and sheltered accommodation; there is also an increase in the number of care homes and nursing homes. The 'grey pound' (the money spent by older populations) has led to new growth industries, e.g. care services, holiday cruises and specialized living aids. The 'grey vote' is also significant in influencing government policy.

Population change and the character of urban and rural areas

Urban areas

Some urban areas have seen massive changes due to redevelopment or migration. In recent years many cities have cleared vast areas of land and built new flats or redeveloped derelict industrial areas to encourage people to live in inner-city areas once again. Migration has also affected cities. Ethnic groups tend to congregate when they first arrive in areas where previous migrants from these groups have settled, and where their own culture, religion and food preferences can be satisfied. As they become more established some migrate out of these original areas, but many prefer to stay here, creating ethnic areas of cities.

Case study: Rusholme, Greater Manchester

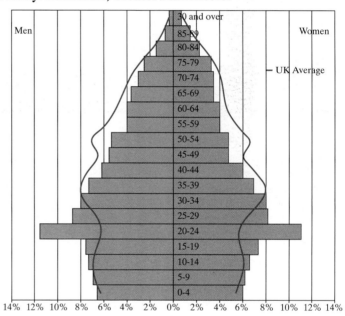

Fig 7
Population pyramid, Rusholme, Manchester

The Rusholme area of Manchester, 3 km from the city centre, contains terraced houses dating back to the late 19th century. They were built for people who worked in the factories in the area and were later used by people who commuted into the city on the cheap trams. This housing was in a poor state of repair by 1960, and was bought up cheaply by landlords to rent out to the new migrants – many of them from Pakistan and Bangladesh – who had come to find work in the city. By the 1970s students had started to move in, as the area is near to the University of Manchester. Some housing was cleared and new social housing replaced it. Some areas were left as open space, others were re-vamped and cleaned up as part of a gentrification process. Many of the shops along Wilmslow Road became curry houses or shops selling goods to the local ethnic groups, such as material for saris and travel agents specializing in trips to Pakistan.

Characteristics of inner cities:

- **Housing**: terraces or flats and a high percentage of rented properties.
- **Age structure**: can be dominated by older people, but where new developments have replaced older properties young adults predominate.
- **Ethnicity**: some areas have a high percentage of one ethnic group.
- **Employment**: often a high number of unemployed or retired people.
- **Wealth**: usually lower income bands.
- **Services**: often poor in terms of GP surgeries and schools, especially in areas which have been redeveloped. Public transport is often good and access to the city centre is easy for shops and jobs.

In Rusholme most of these characteristics can be found, although service provision in terms of health and education is good.

Ethnic group		Central Rusholme	Manchester Metropolitan District
All People	Count	1399	392819
White: British	%	52.47	74.46
White: Irish	%	4.07	3.77
Asian or Asian British: Indian	%	3.36	1.48
Asian or Asian British: Pakistani	%	8.01	5.88
Asian or Asian British: Bangladeshi	%	7.72	0.93
Asian or Asian British: Other Asian	%	3.29	0.84
Black or Black British: Caribbean	%	3.15	2.3
Black or Black British: African	%	4.93	1.69
Economic activity all people	People aged 16-74: Economically active: Unemployed	%	5.19	5.02
Economic activity all people	People aged 16-74: Economically inactive: Retired	%	5.19	10.24
Economic activity all people	People aged 16-74: Economically inactive: Student	%	35.41	12.3

Social welfare

This refers to the opportunities that people have to live in a free and safe environment with access to services and jobs. This may not be equally available to all in all areas. Concentrations of one age group, ethnic group or social class can help to develop a community where people are supportive of each other. It can also concentrate areas of poor housing, unemployment and lack of services such as schools and health facilities, which leads to areas of deprivation.

Essential notes

'Studentification' of an area is where many properties are rented by students. It is usually an area of older housing near to a university. While this may benefit local services and shops, e.g fast food outlets, and allow for the improvement of some properties, it can cause problems for local residents because of noise at unsocial hours; students may leave outside areas of properties untidy, leading to problems of rubbish and overgrown gardens. Landlords are less inclined to improve the appearance of student lets and it can contribute to the area looking run-down.

Table 1
Ethnicity and economic activity data: central Rusholme and Manchester Metropolitan District

Examiners' notes

You need to study two of the following areas: an inner-city area, suburban area, rural urban fringe, rural settlement. For each of your areas of study, investigate the provision of local schools, health facilities, leisure facilities, transport facilities, and anything else that affects how people lead their lives.

Population change and the character of rural areas

Rural areas

Rural areas in more remote locations are declining. There are multiple effects of this decline:

- Older people are left behind as younger people out-migrate to find jobs.
- Village schools close due to a lack of pupils leading to further out-migration of the young.
- Social deprivation due to a lack of services: post offices and food shops close. Access to healthcare becomes more difficult, requiring long journeys.
- Public transport becomes infrequent.
- Few social activities locally, without people to organise them or provide funding.
- Housing is sometimes bought as second homes. These are only inhabited in the tourist season so do not add to the local community.
- Population structure shows a narrow base. There is a low birth rate and there are gaps in the 20–35 years population due to out-migration. There are larger numbers of people over 65.

Some rural areas, with good access, are expanding. They have kept their services, such as the village school and local health centre. There is a large enough community to support local shops, a post office and social amenities. The Postbus service has provided local transport in some areas. The population structure of these areas includes fewer elderly people, a bulge in the 30–50 year population, who often commute long distances to work. There is also a higher birth rate – shown by the expanding base of the pyramid representing the young families of this age group.

Effects of rural expansion:

- New housing estates are built, but often local people cannot afford to buy these houses.
- There is increasing pressure on services such as the local primary school.
- Commuting means that people are absent during the day so the village is empty.
- Changes in life style and culture, brought in by the newcomers, may be resented by locals.

The Isle of Purbeck, Dorset, provides an example of a rural settlement area. This is an isolated area on a peninsula south of Poole harbour, on the south coast of England. There is only one major town, Swanage, and one main road, the A351, which links the area to Bournemouth and Poole.

Characteristics of the Isle of Purbeck:

- Older population with 21.7% over 65 (2001 census)
- Fewer young adults and a lower birth rate
- House prices which have risen more than the national average
- Lower wages than urban areas and few job opportunities

- Housing mostly owner-occupied
- Decline in rural services including local shops, post offices, pubs and petrol stations
- Community centres, churches and schools still functioning in the villages
- Tourism supporting the local economy
- Limited public transport – few local bus services
- Commuting, especially to Poole/Bournemouth for jobs
- Problems of traffic congestion, especially in the summer when tourists and commuters try to use the only main road in the area
- Retirement area: more pressure on local services
- Housing costs: too high for local people, especially due to second-home market
- Some new social housing in Corfe Castle.

Fig 8
The town of Swanage, at the eastern end of the Isle of Purbeck

Population and resources

Overpopulation is where the population is too large for the resources available. It depends on the level of technology available to help to make good use of resources, the climate, and physical limitations of the area. It can cause unemployment and out-migration. This is typical of population pyramids with wide bases and high birth rates where population is still increasing quickly. Resources cannot keep up with population growth, e.g. Bangladesh, Niger.

Underpopulation exists where there are not enough people living in an area or country to utilize resources efficiently. More people might mean a higher standard of living. These areas have in-migration and low unemployment. This is typical of some developed countries with dome-shaped population pyramids, low population growth, and where population density is low, e.g. New Zealand, Norway, Canada.

Optimum population is where the resources available can be developed efficiently to satisfy the needs of the current population and provide the highest standard of living. This is a concept that is rarely achieved.

Population theories have been put forward to explain the relationship between population and resources, which is seen as difficult to keep in balance.

The case for optimism: Ester Boserup

Technology can stretch the limits for production of more resources in order to support growing populations. As demand increases new ideas for greater food production evolve to supply it, e.g. reducing the amount of fallow land to increase production, the use of fertilisers and pesticides, farming new lands like the US prairies, and the use of GM crops.

Julian Simon and **Bjorn Lomborg** add that ideas about technology damaging the environment are not well founded and that more technology should be allowed to help poorer countries to improve their living standards.

The case for pessimism: Thomas Malthus

Malthus pointed out in 1798 that population growth was geometric (2, 4, 8, 16 etc.) while food supply could only grow arithmetically (1, 2, 3, 4) so the world would quickly run out of food for its fast-growing population. He suggested that to balance this shortfall famine, war and disease would increase death rates and reduce mouths to feed, unless the birth rate was reduced by celibacy and later marriage.

In 1972 'The Limits to Growth' report produced by the **neo-Malthusian** Club of Rome suggested that there would be a sudden decline in population in 100 years due to overuse of resources. The report claimed that the spread of famine and war in the Sahel in sub-Saharan Africa was due to population outstripping the ability of the land to support it. The population then decreased as a result and is back in balance with the land. Others say that pollution and global warming, produced by people trying to stretch resources, will eventually create checks on further growth.

Essential notes

Concepts of ideal population numbers for any country are affected by new technology and resources becoming available as well as increasing globalization.

Examiners' notes

You may be asked to evaluate these theories on population and their relationship to resources. Make sure you can put both sides of the argument and assess the validity of these ideas today by using current examples.

They argue that it is not possible to develop sustainably and prevent these disasters.

Sustainability: there have been various attempts to manage population change indirectly in order to achieve sustainable development. These have included preventing pollution and reducing poverty.

Agenda 21 is the UN sustainable development programme agreed at Earth Summits to encourage local authorities to introduce recycling, energy efficiencies and to improve public transport.

Population policies

Governments can intervene to try to alter population structure. For example, they can encourage either higher or lower birth rates, and they can raise the age of retirement or change migration policy.

Case study: China (anti-natalist)

China's historically large population increased following 1950s and 60s policies that encouraged large families in order to increase the workforce. There was a major famine and Chinese authorities realized that China was unable to support such a large population. In 1982 the **one-child policy** was introduced to dramatically reduce population. Incentives were paid to people who followed the policy. Contraceptive advice was free, and the 'granny police' encouraged people to keep to the one-child ideal, sometimes reporting those who might be pregnant and encouraging them to have an abortion. It was considered to be unpatriotic to break these rules and have more than one child, and in many cases large fines were imposed. In rural areas many children 'disappeared' and there were problems with infanticide (baby girls were abandoned to die) because many parents wanted a boy to work the farm. This skewed the population structure as there are more males aged 10 to 30 than females, which has wide implications for the next generation.

Case study: France (pro-natalist)

Since the Second World War France has had low birth and fertility rates. France has high literacy rates and a high standard of living. It faces concerns about a lack of working population and, more recently, its ability to cope with the larger numbers of elderly. It has recently raised the retirement age from 60 to 62 to cope with this, leading to strikes (October 2010). Successive governments have put in place policies to encourage higher birth rates, e.g. free places at nurseries (so that women can return to work) and tax benefits and cash incentives for a third child. The fertility rate has increased from 1.71 in 1995 to 1.98 in 2006.

Essential notes

Sustainability is 'development that meets the needs of the present without compromising the ability of future generations to meet their own needs', Bruntland Report 1987.

Essential notes

In some countries control of migration was the key to controlling population structure; e.g. the USA imposed limits on immigration. The Philippines encouraged emigration. Indonesia encouraged transmigration to less populated areas, at first by force and now out of economic necessity following the exploitation of natural resources and labour needs.

Examiners' notes

Learn how to describe a global distribution from a world map. Use reference points such as: tropical, equatorial, northern hemisphere, and continental areas (e.g. SE Asia).

Global patterns of food supply, consumption and trade

World food production continues to increase, yet the rate at which it is increasing has slowed. From 1970 to 1990, world grain production grew by 64%. From 1990 to 2009, it increased by only 24%.

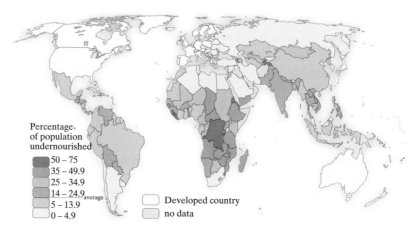

Fig 1
World percentage of undernourished population

The world has made significant progress in raising food consumption per person. The growth in food consumption has been accompanied by a change in diet away from staples such as roots and tubers towards more livestock products and vegetable oils.

Trade adds to domestic supplies of food to meet consumption needs; it reduces supply variability, though not necessarily price instability; it encourages economic growth; it makes efficient use of world resources; and it permits global production to take place in those regions most suited to it.

World food trade is complex. One example is the trade in wheat.

Examiners' notes

Describe the pattern of trade in wheat shown in fig 2. Also, prepare another case study of a traded food commodity, e.g. bananas. Be able to describe where they come from, where they go, general patterns and any anomalies. Use resources such as the UN Food and Agriculture Organisation (FAO) (www.fao.org/corp/statistics/en/).

Fig 2
Top wheat importers and exporters, 2007 (%)

The geopolitics of food

The value of the global trade in food is almost $1 000bn. It represents about 12% of the value of all global trade. Each country wishes to extract the best deal from their trading, whether from imports or exports. Richer countries are able to make trade deals which mean that the farmers of developing countries do not always get fair prices for their products. Some developed countries protect their own farmers by subsidizing them; developing countries are unable to do this. The **World Trade Organization (WTO)** is the only global international organization dealing with the rules of trade.

Contrasting agricultural food production systems

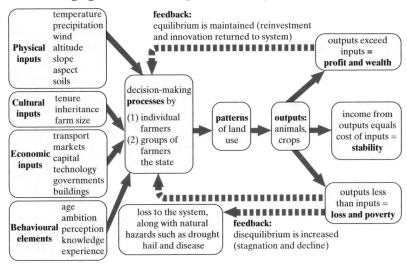

Fig 3
Decision-making processes in agricultural food production systems

Farms can be considered as **open systems**. The inputs include physical, cultural, economic and behavioural. Generally, as an area develops the physical factors become less important as the human inputs increase.

Food production systems can include a combination of:

commercial	intensive	arable (growing crops)
or	or	or
subsistence	extensive	livestock (raising animals)
		or
		mixed (growing crops and raising animals)

Intensive farming is usually relatively small scale and can either be:

- **Capital intensive:** Money is invested in soil improvement, machinery, buildings, pest control, high quality seeds/animals. There are few people employed and so output is high per hectare and per worker, e.g. tomato production in the Netherlands.

- **Labour intensive:** The number of farm workers is high and so there is a high output per hectare but a low output per worker, e.g. rice cultivation in the Ganges valley.

- **Extensive:** Farming is carried out on a large scale over a large area. This varies greatly. There are areas where, although the labour force is low, there is a high capital input, such as on quality seeds/animals, or pesticides and insecticides, e.g. wheat farming in the Canadian prairies. Other areas still have a low labour force but rely on the sheer amount of land they are farming to provide sufficient output for their needs, e.g. sheep ranching in Australia.

Managing food supply: increasing production

Food security

The World Food Summit of 1996 defined **food security** as existing 'when all people at all times have access to sufficient, safe, nutritious food to maintain a healthy and active life'. It can also be defined as including both physical and economic access to food that meets people's dietary needs as well as their food preferences.

To improve global food security, there have been several strategies adopted. These include the **Green Revolution** and the use of **genetic modification (GM)**.

The Green Revolution

This was a term coined by the US Agency for International Development. It was a movement to increase crop yields by using:

- New crop varieties, known as high yield varieties (HYVs), that had been developed to produce high yields per hectare
- Irrigation
- Fertilizers
- Pesticides
- Mechanization

The Green Revolution started in Mexico in 1943 but came to real prominence in India in the 1960s. By 1968, India had adopted IR8, a hybrid rice plant that had been developed at the International Rice Research Institute in the Philippines. This could yield up to 10 times more than traditional varieties of rice. It has been most successful in Asia where 90% of all wheat and 66% of rice is produced using HYVs.

There are many disadvantages to the Green Revolution, including that:

- Costly inputs of fertilizers and pesticides have led some farmers into debt.
- The HYVs require more weed control.
- Mechanization has led to rural unemployment and rural–urban migration.

The genetic modification (GM) of crops and animals

Unlike the production of hybrid plants and animals by **selective breeding**, genetic modification entails taking genes (a unit of heredity) from one species and adding them to the DNA (the genetic instructions used in the development and functioning of all known living organisms) of another species. The resultant plant or animal will have some of the characteristics of the donor plant or animal in its make-up.

An example of GM: Scientists have transferred a gene to the oilseed rape plant which enables the plant to resist a certain pesticide. When farmers spray the genetically modified rape crop with pesticides, they can destroy most of the pests without killing the rape plants.

- *Advantages:* The farmer can grow more, because it is easier to fight pests. The farmer also uses less crop spray (which itself can be environmentally friendly).

- *Disadvantages:* Genes from the GM rape crop could be transferred to pests. The pests then become resistant to the crop spray. Rape plants can also pollinate weeds which could then acquire pesticide resistance.

Other high-technology approaches to increasing food supply

Cloning: Cloning is used in agriculture to produce identical reproductions of a crop. An entire crop of healthy, prosperous plants can be cloned from one strong parent plant. Recently, cloning of animals has become an **issue**. Some breeders want to use cloning to copy elite animals, using them as breeding stock to upgrade entire herds.

Land colonization: In Brazil, poor farmers are encouraged by government land policies to settle on forest lands. Each squatter acquires the right to continue using a piece of land by living on a plot of unclaimed public land (no matter how marginal the land) and 'using' it for at least one year and a day. After five years the squatter acquires ownership and hence the right to sell the land. The land is planted with crops like bananas, palms, manioc, maize, or rice. After a year or two, the productivity of the soil declines, and the farmers clear new forest for more short-term agricultural land. The old, now infertile fields are used for small-scale cattle grazing or left for waste.

Land reform: This generally entails the transfer of ownership of land from large (often absent) landowners to smaller resident farmers. Ownership tends to encourage farmers to invest in the land. Examples of land reform can be found in Bolivia, Brazil and India. In Russia the reforms involve the transfer of farmland ownership from the state to individuals.

Commercialization: In some countries there has been a drive towards the production of cash crops (e.g. coffee, cotton, groundnuts) at the expense of the traditional subsistence farming. This can have huge effects on local economies when small farmers become the victim of changing world markets and prices.

Appropriate/intermediate technology solutions: In developing countries, technology has been developed that poorly educated farmers can learn to use and become self-sufficient in. Two examples of this are:

- **Drip irrigation:** In Zimbabwe, US aid agencies have distributed drip irrigation kits to 24 000 small farmers. Designed to save labour and water, enhance nutrition and improve food security, the average drip-irrigation kit is easy to install. The surplus vegetables produced by drip irrigation have generated enough income to buy a year's worth of corn (maize), pay for schooling or buy basic medicines.

- **Stone lines:** This is an even simpler technology used in parts of Burkina Faso. Lines of stones are placed across hillsides. When the rains arrive, the water washes down the slope and is caught by the lines of stones. Any soil carried by the water is caught also.

Managing food supply: controlling production

The European Union

The European Union (EU) is an economic and political union of 27 states throughout Europe. These countries have several common policies. One of the most important is the **Common Agricultural Policy (CAP)**. The aim of the CAP is to provide farmers with a reasonable standard of living, to provide consumers with quality food at fair prices, and to preserve rural heritage. It is very expensive, costing 43.8 billion, representing nearly 31% of the total EU budget in 2010.

The CAP originally offered subsidies and systems guaranteeing high prices to farmers, providing incentives for them to produce more essential foodstuffs and so controlling the nature of the food produced.

One of these policies was the introduction of **intervention prices**. When the market price for a commodity fell to a set level the EU would buy the entire production at the intervention price. The farmers were guaranteed a reasonable price for their produce whether or not it could be sold on the open market.

Although at first successful, this policy led to surpluses and the accumulation of the notorious milk 'lakes' and butter, beef and grain 'mountains'. These surplus stocks were expensive to keep and so were sold to non-EU countries at much reduced prices.

There have been several policy changes in recent years designed to reduce this overproduction and yet maintain farm incomes. These include:

- **Subsidies:** The vast majority of aid to farmers is now paid independently of how much they produce. Under the new system farmers still receive direct income payments to maintain income stability, but the link to production has been cut. This subsidy has taken the form of a single farm payment for EU farmers, linked to: the respecting of environmental standards; food safety; animal and plant health; animal welfare standards; the requirement to keep all farmland in good agricultural and environmental condition. Cutting the link between subsidies and production will enable EU farmers to be more market-orientated. They will be free to produce according to what is most profitable for them while still enjoying a required stability of income.
- **Quotas:** Fixed quotas on milk production were introduced in the early 1980s, with penalties for overproduction.
- **Set-aside:** This was, at first, introduced on a voluntary basis in 1988. It then became compulsory in 1992. Set-aside obliged farmers to leave a percentage of their land uncultivated. Although it achieved some environmental benefits, the policy was suspended in 2008 following a series of poor cereal harvests. There are complicated rules regarding the use of set-aside land. UK farmers are allowed to move their designated set-aside land each year or can keep just one area as set-aside. The land can be cultivated for oilseed rape or willow coppicing (willow is becoming an important biofuel).

The main requirement is that the land must be available for re-cultivation if cereal production needs to be increased.

- **Tariffs:** A tariff is a tax levied on imports or exports. The EU applies these to specific goods imported into the EU. These are set to control consumption of certain foodstuffs by raising the price. They also have been used to favour or help some overseas producers by giving them lower tariffs. For example, former colonies of EU member states (e.g. Dominica) had lower tariffs to pay on exporting their bananas to the EU than the main South American banana-producing countries. This effectively gave the former colonies a trading advantage. In recent years this preferential treatment has been much reduced.

As a result of all these initiatives the surpluses of the late twentieth century have been reduced. Two examples are given in **fig 4**, butter and beef.

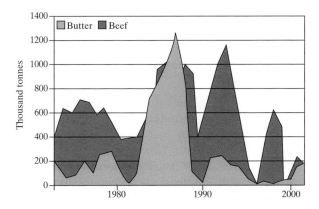

Fig 4
Beef and butter mountains

Examiners' notes

Many examination questions ask candidates to 'evaluate' or to 'assess the extent to which' a scheme has been successful. A description of the changing sizes of food surpluses would be one way of measuring the extent to which the EU policies have been successful.

Environmental Stewardship: The Environmental Stewardship scheme (ESS) was launched in March 2005. It was designed to build upon the work of other schemes such as the **Environmentally Sensitive Areas** scheme. Its main aims are to:

- Conserve wildlife and biodiversity
- Maintain and enhance landscape quality and character
- Protect the historic environment and natural resources
- Promote public access and understanding of the countryside
- Provide flood management
- Conserve genetic resources

There are different levels of stewardship, each of which comes with a different grant. Farmers who gain the **Higher Level Stewardship** grant have to have completed initiatives such as:

- Providing buffer zones around fields
- Maintenance of hedgerows, ponds and heathland
- Maintenance and restoration of species-rich semi-natural grassland or wet grassland

Essential notes

Environmental stewardship is a policy that, although not specifically designed to reduce surpluses, is having an effect on production. This is because its main feature is a grant paid direct to a farmer regardless of how much they grow.

Changes in demand

High value food exports from poorer countries to richer developed markets

Demand for fresh fruit and vegetables has increased in the UK. This is partly due to increasing wealth, but also initiatives like the UK government's 'five-a-day' campaign. Many consumers, also, have lost the link between the time of year and the availability of seasonal produce. This has led to increasing demand for exotic fruit and vegetables as well as familiar varieties at any time of year.

The UK imported around 0.78 million tonnes (mt) of fresh fruit and vegetables from African nations in 2005. These goods had a value of £495m. This has been growing at 1.1% per year.

An example of a country exporting to the UK is Kenya. Leguminous vegetables (e.g. mange tout) constitute the largest proportion of these exports. The vegetable exports have grown from 3 800 tonnes in 1988 to 25 000 tonnes in 2005, worth about £71m. Most of these are highly perishable and very valuable. This means they are transported by air. This has led to concerns about the **carbon footprint** of this food and has led to the concept of **food miles**.

The Kenyan farmers' main problems are caused by their production being affected by unfavourable weather and changes in consumer demand that make their markets unstable, create insecurity, and make their incomes unpredictable. Alongside this, many farmers have given up growing their traditional crops, which led, in 2009, to food shortages being reported by the Kenyan government. Advantages of the exports are that valuable foreign currency is brought to Kenya and can be used in development from local to national levels.

Increasing demand for organic products

The market for organic produce in the UK in 2008 was £2.1bn, up from £600m in 2001. This demand rose rapidly through the early 21st century, but has slowed down to an increase of only 1.7% per year. The fact that the sales of organic fruit, bread and confectionary fell rapidly from 2007 to 2008 tends to show that organic food is perceived as a luxury item that can be dispensed with during times of economic hardship.

Moves towards sourcing food locally/regionally

One way to reduce food miles is to obtain food from local sources. For example, Tesco has pledged to cut down on its food miles by opening six regional offices in England and Wales, responsible for buying food from local farmers. It will allow much smaller producers to do business with Britain's biggest retailer.

Another movement in the UK towards sourcing food locally is through **farmers' markets**. A farmers' market is one in which farmers, growers or producers from a defined local area are present in person to sell their own produce direct to the public. All products sold should have been grown, reared, caught, brewed, pickled, baked, smoked or processed by the stallholder.

Examiners' notes

Prepare a case study of one example of farming in a developing country that has been changed from traditional agriculture to high value cash crops.

Examiners' notes

In the UK the Soil Association is responsible for certifying organic food. Their website (www.soilassociation.org) gives detailed information about organic food demand and production. Remember, it offers only a one-sided view of the benefits of organic farming. Research an alternative view.

Examiners' notes

Make a case study of your own family. Find out details of where their food is sourced, how much of it is imported, organic, sourced locally etc.

Food supplies in a globalizing economy

Globalization is defined by the UK government as: 'the growing interdependence and interconnectedness of the modern world through increased flows of goods, services, capital, people and information'.

The growth of **transnational corporations** (**TNCs**) in food production demonstrates this well. These are very powerful firms that have business activities in more than one country. For example:

- Cargill, Archer Daniels and Bunge control nearly 90% of global grain trade.
- DuPont and Monsanto dominate the global seed market.

These large TNCs have succeeded through integration, market capture, and sheer size in gaining the ability to alter the market price of their products. Within the food supply industry, there are high levels of both horizontal and vertical integration. Horizontal integration occurs when there are few firms operating at any one point in the supply chain (e.g. coffee growing); vertical integration occurs when a number of firms dominate more than one area on the supply chain (e.g. growing, shipping, and canning one product).

Critics say:

- TNCs have the power to pressurize certain countries or regions to produce food that does not meet their population's needs.
- TNCs push farmers' profits and farm workers' wages so low that they cannot feed themselves or their families.
- Their operations use a lot of chemical fertilizers, pesticides and GM crops.

The TNCs on the other hand, argue that they are environmentally responsible and have their farmers' interest at heart. Unilever, an Anglo-Dutch TNC, claims:

- It has led a campaign in Kenya to educate all their employees about the dangers and prevention of the spread of HIV/AIDS.
- It is committed to source all its palm oil (an ingredient of margarine and cooking oils) from certified sustainable sources by 2015.
- Around 50% of the tea for its Lipton Yellow Label and PG Tips tea bags in western Europe was sourced from Rainforest Alliance Certified farms, making progress towards a target of buying all its tea from sustainable sources.

Environmental aspects of global trade in foodstuffs

Apart from the food miles and carbon footprint created by the international trade in foodstuffs, there are other environmental impacts. For example, palm oil plantations have been associated with problems of:

- Habitat conversion, particularly of tropical forests
- Soil erosion and degradation
- Threats to key species
- Effluents from processing

Examiners' notes

It is important to have a case study of one TNC that is involved in the food industry. Find out how many countries it operates in, what its main raw agricultural products are and into what final products they are converted.

Examiners' notes

Build into your case study of a TNC any aspect of how it has had an effect on the environment.

Examiners' notes

The role of TNCs in food production is an issue. There are many pressure groups (e.g. Corporate Watch and Sustainable Stuff) that criticize the TNCs. Investigate one of these pressure groups. What are their main grievances, and what do the TNCs say in reply?

The potential for sustainable food supplies

'A sustainable agricultural system is one that can indefinitely meet the requirements for food and fibre at socially acceptable, economical and environmental costs.' Crossen (1992)

This means that land is maintained in such a way that it can be used by future generations in the same way.

In the EU, **integrated crop management** (ICM) is a system that is being investigated to see whether it can help commercial farmers become sustainable. It is a method of farming that balances the requirements of running a profitable business with responsibility and sensitivity to the environment. It includes practices that avoid waste, enhance energy efficiency and minimise pollution. It combines the best of modern technology with some basic principles of good farming practice and is a whole-farm, long-term strategy. For example, it encourages:

- The use of crop rotations
- Appropriate cultivation techniques
- Careful choice of seed varieties
- Minimum reliance on artificial fertiliser, pesticides and fossil fuels
- Maintenance of the landscape
- The enhancement of wildlife habitats.

Examples of this are: citrus fruit production in Spain and arable farming in Germany.

Case study: a sustainable system in a developing country

In developing countries many subsistence farmers do not have many choices: they have to be sustainable or there will be a food shortage.

Examiners' notes

The European Commission is a good source of information on ICM schemes. Using the model of the farm as system, make notes on one example of ICM.

Examiners' notes

The case study of the Dogon Plateau can be used as an example of sustainable food production or as one case study of an approach to managing food supply. The specification states that another, contrasting case study should be carried out. Use a commercial case study in a developed country.

Fig 5
The Dogon Plateau, Mali

The Dogon Plateau, Mali, is a low rainfall area, and the lack of rainfall has become an even more severe problem. The annual average rainfall has diminished from 555 mm to as little as 465 mm in recent years. Crop yields have suffered, and water has become scarce. Streams dry up earlier in the season, and the water tables have gradually fallen – which means that wells and boreholes have to be dug ever deeper and deeper.

As well as being low, the overall rainfall is also unreliable and individual rainstorms can be very intense. There is considerable runoff from the rocky surfaces. This leads to erosion of soil on the fields below. Wind erosion is also a serious problem here during the dry season.

The Dogon depend principally on their subsistence food crops. Most of the land cultivated is planted with sorghum and millet. Groundnuts are also common. In addition, irrigated vegetable production is important close to the water courses. The most common vegetable here is onions.

The Dogon use a variety of traditional soil and water conservation practices. These include:

- **Stone lines:** These are placed across low-angled hill slopes. They reduce rainfall runoff and reduce soil erosion. These lines of stones are 20 cm in height.
- **Earth mounds:** These are constructed between plants to help slow runoff, as well as acting as small compost heaps, improving soil fertility. The mounds are constructed during the first weeding in July when weeds are scraped together and covered with earth. The next season's seeds are planted into what remains of the mounds where the fertility of the soil has been improved.
- **Small terraces:** These are made by the sides of watercourses where water is available, but there is no soil. A network of small stone squares is built on the bare rock and, after being filled with earth, is planted with onions or another vegetable crop. Manure is added. They are **irrigated** from the nearby streams.
- **Live fences:** These are planted to protect fields from animals and to act as a barrier to runoff. Euphorbia is planted because it can also be used to provide fuel.

The people of the Dogon Plateau have maintained this way of life for generations. It remains to be seen whether it can be maintained following the effects of recent climate change and an increasing demand from a growing population.

Essential notes

To help learn the case study of the Dogon Plateau, convert the information given here, and any personal research, into a farm systems diagram. Break it down into inputs, processes and outputs.

Types of energy

Non-renewable resources (also known as stock/finite/capital resources) have built up slowly over long periods of geological time and they are being used up quickly. They are mainly fossil fuels but also include uranium used in nuclear power.

Coal: formed from swamp forests which grew in carboniferous times. Coal formed in seams which are often now deep below ground, so it is expensive to mine. Any coal found at the surface can be quarried out cheaply so the easy-to-mine deposits were exploited first.

Oil: formed from the remains of microscopic sea creatures trapped in sediments. The oil percolated upwards within pores in porous rocks until it reached an impermeable cap rock which held the oil in a reservoir.

Natural gas: given off as oil forms. It is less dense than oil so rises to the top of the porous rocks.

Renewable resources (also known as flow resources/income resources) are available as continuous flow (non-critical resources) which does not run out, e.g. solar power, or as critical resources such as wood, which has to be managed to ensure that current consumption does not outstrip renewal rates.

Sustainable development involves managing resources to ensure that current exploitation of any energy resources does not compromise the supply of energy for future generations.

Reserves are the proportion of a resource which can be developed and used with currently available technology.

Recoverable reserves are able to be estimated at known locations and are likely to be extracted in the near future.

Speculative reserves have not yet been explored, but are in places where geology suggests there may be deposits.

Primary energy resources are natural resources, e.g. oil, which may be converted to more useful manufactured products, such as petrol for use in energy production, which are then classed as **secondary energy resources**.

Energy in the UK

Primary energy sources include coal, oil and gas. The UK was self-reliant for energy production from the mid 1990s to 2004. There are still large reserves of coal, e.g. at Daw Mill colliery near Coventry. At present many mines are not thought to be economically viable due to deep and fractured seams, the coal being sulphurous (causing acid rain), and cheaper coal being imported from Australia and Poland. Oil and gas are found under the North Sea. They are now reduced and will eventually run out, although new small reserves are still being found. Oil is used for transport, and gas, being a cleaner burning fuel, to produce electricity. Renewable sources supply only 7% of UK energy; nuclear ranged between 12 and 18% between 2000 and 2009, but this will decrease if nuclear plants begin to close as they became obsolete or need renewing. The government is considering plans to build new nuclear plants on old sites to fill the energy gap.

There is a target of 15% of energy to come from renewable sources by 2015 to reduce carbon emissions and to help prevent global warming. The main renewables in the UK are:

- **Biofuels** – especially gas from landfill sites, waste burning and sewage gas. A small amount is from wood.
- **HEP** – most are large-scale schemes in Scotland, including some pumped storage schemes, but most feasible sites have already been used. Small-scale schemes are now being set up but even then only about 3% of energy needs would come from HEP.
- **Wind power** – in 2010 there were 2 976 wind turbines producing enough power to run approximately 2.6 m homes. Some are offshore, such as the Rhyl flats wind farm 8 km off the coast of North Wales near Abergele which has 25 turbines. There is controversy about the location of wind farms such as this one as they spoil the view out to sea (see **fig 6**)and could be a hazard to ships, and some say they disturb bird movements. Onshore sites also receive many objections such as those on Scout Moor near Rochdale.

There are plans to build **tidal barrages** and to install solar panels on houses. More efficient ways of producing and transporting energy, e.g. combined heat and power stations which reuse waste heat from the generation process, should reduce some losses; better technology and insulation will help to reduce the amount of fuel needed.

Energy mix
The energy mix of a country is the proportions of different sources of energy used by households, industry and business together with that used in electricity generation. In the UK the energy mix has changed from a dominance of coal to a dominance of oil and then to gas; although renewables are increasing, nuclear power is still important for base load.

Essential notes
Electricity is produced constantly by base load power stations which form the mainstay of power supply in most developed countries. Surpluses can be sold abroad (from the UK to France for instance) or can be used by pumped storage HEP stations, such as Dinorwic in North Wales, to pump water into an upper reservoir at night ready to top up electricity supply for peak demand at breakfast time the next day.

Examiners' notes
You should compare the changing energy mix in at least one other country (such as in the USA, India or Kenya) with that of the UK.

Fig 1
Scout Moor Wind Farm near Rochdale

Essential notes
The government's fuel mix website provides information about the energy resources used to generate the electricity supplied into the power grid in the UK: www. decc.gov.uk/en/content/cms/ statistics/fuel_mix/fuel_mix

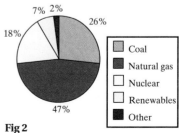

Fig 2
Fuel mix for all UK electricity suppliers 2009–10

Essential notes

Risks to oil supplies:

- China, India and other newly industrializing countries (NICs) will increase the demand for energy from dwindling supplies. This could lead to conflict and higher prices.
- Iraq, a major producer, has economic problems and is politically unstable.
- Terrorist threats could make trade with the West more difficult.
- OPEC could raise prices.
- Russia controls many power sources and may want to exert greater political influence.

Global patterns

Energy supply, consumption and trade

Most resources are concentrated in very few countries.

Oil: reserves are mainly in the Middle East (especially Saudi Arabia), Russia and the former Russian states, e.g. Kazakhstan, with the USA producing a large amount of its own. Greatest consumption is in Europe, Asia and North America, especially the USA. This results in crude oil being moved from African and Middle Eastern countries into those of the newly industrializing and the more developed world. It is estimated that there are known reserves for the next 40 years. Most is transported the long distances by tanker but there are numerous short-distance pipelines. OPEC (the Organization of Petroleum Exporting Countries) represents 12 countries, mostly in the Middle East and controlling 37% of world production (2008). Oil prices have risen because:

- OPEC control prices and set quotas for production.
- There are fears of political instability, e.g. in Nigeria.
- Since the recent recession exchange rates of the euro and dollar are lower, making oil more expensive.
- Oil companies now work with lower stocks, which raises demand.
- Demand from China's industrialization programme and ever rising demand from the USA have pushed prices up. On the other hand, the high price has allowed once uneconomic oilfields to be developed.

Natural gas: has a wider distribution and reserves should last for approximately 70 years. Russia has the largest reserves, followed by Iran. It is a cleaner fuel but is flammable and is often transported as liquefied natural gas (LNG). Some producing areas transport gas by pipeline (e.g. from the former Russian states to eastern Europe and from the North Sea fields to Easington in the UK) but maintenance costs are high. Production of natural gas tends to be nearer to the main markets. Global natural gas production has increased by 2.5% over the past 10 years.

Coal: is more widely available and should last for at least 150 years. In China and India coal is cheap to mine but it has a high sulphur content. Most developed countries have supplies of coal – it was one reason for the Industrial Revolution beginning in these countries. Many coalfields are not economically viable at present and coalmining has declined in many EU countries. In the UK coal declined mainly because the easily accessible coal had already been mined and mechanization was difficult in fractured and faulted seams. In addition, labour costs were high and government policy was to move to natural gas. Globally, it is still the major fuel for generating electricity (92% in Poland and South Africa) and for steel making.

Uranium: the fuel for nuclear power. The largest amounts are found in the USA, Canada and Australia. There was a reluctance to support a nuclear industry following the accident at Chernobyl in 1986, and in the UK many older power stations were not renewed as they became obsolete. There are also issues of security and the disposal of nuclear waste. With increasing demand for energy, together with issues such as the depletion of fossil fuels, carbon dioxide emissions and acid rain, governments are looking to nuclear fuel to provide base load power. Nuclear power is important in the USA, Japan, the UK and France. Developing countries like India and NICs like South Korea have also developed nuclear power.

TNCs and the oil trade

Transnational corporations, such as BP, have production facilities in many countries but research and development (R&D) facilities tend to be in the more developed nations. Their global impact results from controlling economic activity in many different countries. They can influence government policy and take advantage of cheap production costs in any country. They have influence over political decisions worldwide.

BP and its subsidiaries operate in more that 100 countries and employ over 100 000 people. It owns, or part-owns, petrol stations, pipelines, retail outlets and refineries. It is exploring new resources in Egypt, Indonesia, Iraq, Jordan, Russia, Angola and the Gulf of Mexico. Being UK-based, BP has its headquarters in London and much of its R&D is in the UK. It has a 13.6% share in a new pipeline moving oil in Iraq, in partnership with the Iraqi state-owned Southern Oil and the China National Petroleum Company. In Angola, BP is working on an LNG pipeline project due to open in 2012.

The geopolitics of energy

Energy supplies are distributed unevenly, and are often a long way from the consumers. Some energy supplies are in politically unstable areas, or are transported through areas where there is conflict. There is a risk of disruption to energy supply (e.g. Ukraine), and environmental damage (e.g. Chernobyl). There is also concern over countries developing nuclear power which could lead to the development of nuclear weapons. India and Pakistan have nuclear power stations but have not signed the Nuclear Non-Proliferation Treaty, and there were worries about Iran building a new nuclear power station at Bashehr. There are disputes over gas supplies to Belarus, and in the case of new oil and gas resources in the Caspian Sea there are worries about disputes between Russia and the newly independent states such as Azerbaijan. A pipeline could pass through Azerbaijan and Georgia, to link these resources to Turkey and the Mediterranean without having to pass through Russia, which could lose Russia export opportunities and control over distribution of these resources, possibly causing conflict.

Cooperation over energy

The G8 group of nations met in St Petersburg in 2006 at the global energy summit. The plan was to work together to increase stability of energy markets, improve investment, diversify energy mix, ensure security of energy infrastructure, reduce energy poverty, and work on sustainable development of energy to address climate change issues. Other cooperative plans include the IPCC Copenhagen Accord on climate change. TNCs such as BP are involved in cooperation with governments and academics to research new energy technologies, e.g. the Energy Biosciences Institute at Berkeley, California.

Essential notes

Ukraine has recently been in dispute with Russia over gas supplies. Gazprom, a Russian company, threatened to raise prices. Ukraine would not pay the increased price, and in January 2006 Russia closed the pipeline to Ukraine. This also affected supplies to the EU, as the pipeline carried one fifth of the EU's gas supply, and caused prices to rise there. The dispute continued but an agreement was reached in April 2010. This is the first time that gas supplies to EU countries were cut and has led EU countries to diversify supply sources.

Essential notes

Carbon dioxide storage is already happening 1 km below the sea bed above the Norwegian Sleipner oilfield a saline aquifer. Visit www. co2storage.co.uk for more information about carbon capture.

Essential notes

The Chernobyl nuclear power plant explosion sent radioactive materials into the high atmosphere which then came down in rain over Scandinavia and western Europe in the following days. This was a global environmental disaster caused by poor maintenance, human error and the disregard of safety rules. Management and safety systems have since been improved in Russia. There are already high standards of safety in the UK and other developed countries, but the disaster made the public worried about the safety of nuclear energy and forced many governments to change energy policy away from nuclear power.

The environmental impact of energy production

All energy production has some impact on the environment, but renewable resources are considered to be less harmful.

Fuel-wood gathering

In many developing countries the main use of energy resources is the consumption of wood for cooking. The removal of woodland for firewood means that there is decreased interception of rainfall which increases run-off and soil erosion, contributing to desertification. It also means that people have to travel longer distances to find supplies. Replanting with fast-growing trees, and the introduction of solar cookers, are initiatives helping to solve this issue.

Nuclear power

Nuclear power produces little carbon dioxide and almost no sulphur dioxide, and there are good reserves of uranium, stretched by the advent of fast breeder reactors. It does, however, produce radioactive waste which remains active for thousands of years, and so must be stored safely. Before selecting a site for waste there needs to be consideration of:

- Geology
- Drainage and water supplies
- Transport
- Pressure groups
- Effects on farming
- Distance from housing
- Effects on tourism and wildlife
- Effects on health
- Possible terrorist attacks

In the UK, storage takes place near Sellafield in Cumbria, where waste is vitrified (converted into glass), sealed in steel-clad containers, and buried deep underground.

Fig 3
Sellafield nuclear power station

Fossil fuels

When burnt, **fossil fuels** produce carbon dioxide which is thought to contribute to **global warming**. This is where atmospheric gases trap heat from the sun inside the earth's atmosphere causing a heating effect on the planet. Effects may include more extreme weather events, sea level rise (from expansion) and possible further rise if ice caps melt. This will have greatest impact on the developing world. The Kyoto Protocol 1997, Bali road map 2007, and the Copenhagen Accord 2009, aim to reduce carbon dioxide emissions. Strategies include:

- **Carbon credits** – tradeable financial certificates earned, for example, by replanting forests
- **Carbon trading** – where a country or company which has met its targets for carbon dioxide reduction can sell any extra reduction to another company or country

Acid rain (deposition) is also produced by the burning of fossil fuels. Sulphur dioxide and carbon dioxide emissions make rainwater more acidic; in some areas where there are high pollution levels rain can be as acidic as pH4. This more acidic rainfall can be moved thousands of miles by the prevailing wind and is alleged to have caused damage to human health, forests, buildings and loss of fish stocks.

The use of lime to reduce the acidity of soils and lakes has been effective in some areas. An EU agreement of 1988 reduced emissions of sulphur dioxide by 58%. Potential exhaustion of fossil fuels means that alternatives are being developed which will reduce the carbon dioxide and sulphur dioxide levels for the future, e.g. renewables. The reduction of consumption through energy efficiency and conservation will also help.

Renewable energy

Biomass: plants and dead vegetable matter which can be converted into biofuels. It includes ethanol production and burning wood, dung, and crop residues; collecting methane from sewage, landfill sites and rotting vegetation. These are all renewable and less polluting than fossil fuels. However, land is taken from food production (see Brazil case study on p 83) often ousting local tenant farmers who then have to find work elsewhere, and it may cause food shortages. It will also require fertilizers and pesticides which are oil derivatives.

Solar power: photovoltaic cells convert solar radiation from daylight (rather than just sunlight) into electrical energy. This is a clean energy, but the outlay cost is high and it would be less cost effective in high latitudes where solar radiation is low. Sanlucar la Mayor near Seville in Spain has an array of solar reflectors which concentrate solar energy on to a collecting tower where water is heated and used to generate steam for electricity production.

Wind energy: this is important in Europe and North America where winds blow strongly enough in winter to develop sufficient power. The energy source is free, non-polluting, does not add to global warming, and farming can continue. Objections are often on the grounds of visual amenity, as some people say they spoil views; other objections are that they are noisy, disturb birds and are expensive to build. Over 7 000 wind turbines are needed to replace the amount of energy produced by one nuclear power station.

☞ This topic continues on the next two pages

Examiners' notes

Make sure that you can give located case studies of environmental effects and that you can name and date some global agreements on energy policies.

Essential notes

The UK produces about 3% of the world's greenhouse gases with 1% of its population.

Essential notes

Acid deposition can be reduced by using:

- Less sulphurous fuels
- 'Scrubbers' to chemically remove pollutant gases
- Natural gas, as a 'cleaner' fuel
- Renewable energy or nuclear power
- Catalytic converters on cars

Essential notes

For more information about solar energy go to: www.solarpaces.org

Essential notes

For more information about Pelamis go to: www.pelamiswave.com

Wave energy: Small-scale schemes have been developed in the UK; for example, Limpet off the island of Islay, Scotland. This started in 2004 when a deep channel was excavated in the sea and a concrete chamber was constructed to hold onshore waves. Trapped air is forced through turbines to generate electricity. The Pelamis 'sea snake' is now ready to produce power from waves. Its bobbing action turns turbines to produce 750kW of power, enough for 500 homes. It has been 'parked' off the coast of the Orkneys at Billia Croo, Hoy.

Fig 4
Pelamis sea snake producing electricity from wave power

Essential notes

There is further information about the proposed Severn barrage at: www.reuk.co.uk/Severn-Barrage-Tidal-Power.htm

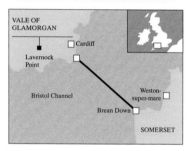

Fig 5
Map showing position of proposed Severn barrage

Tidal energy: this involves the creation of energy where there is a large tidal range, e.g. the Atlantic coast of Europe. The estuary of the river Rance in Brittany, France has a tidal barrage (1966) and one has been discussed for the river Severn estuary in the UK, although the government decided not to go ahead. The Severn has a tidal range of 14 m and a 16 km barrage would have interrupted the tidal race from Brean Down to Lavernock Point, allowing water to be held behind it. It would have had 214 turbines generating 8.6 MW during flow. It would have required a new road link and locks would have been constructed to allow shipping to pass through. Environmental groups argued that the barrage would reduce biodiversity (redshanks and shelducks) and destroy 75% of their habitat. Silting up behind the barrage and increased erosion and flooding further along the estuary were also considered risks.

Other renewables: includes geothermal energy. This involves producing power from the hot rocks which are found near to the surface in geologically active areas of the world, such as Iceland. Water coming into contact with these hot rocks is naturally turned into steam which can be used to generate power which is clean and renewable.

Appropriate technology

In developing countries intermediate technology is used to help to increase energy supplies. This includes solar cookers, methane gas from local sewage plants or animal dung, the use of biomass and solar panels. These help to produce cheap and sustainable energy, including electricity. Bicycles might be used to improve transport connections; improvement in local bus services would make long distance travel cheap and sustainable.

Examiners' notes

Remember that in developing countries in the past, large energy-producing schemes were often funded by more developed nations and then used to provide cheap power for large western-owned factories. Recent developments have been small scale and local and these make more of an impact on the lives of local people.

Case study: managing energy supply, bioethanol in Brazil

Brazil has cultivated sugar cane for many years. When the price of oil rose in 1973 the country decided to reduce its reliance on imports of energy, especially oil. Brazil explored for oil and gas in its own territory and also developed HEP. Brazilians then looked to develop biofuels, using sugar cane to produce ethanol to be used as a fuel in cars and lorries. The PROALCOOL programme took control of all sugar cane production for making ethanol. This had the effect of displacing tenant farmers and causing migration to the cities.

The government banned the use of diesel-powered vehicles and ensured that government agencies bought ethanol-powered cars. Import duties remained high on petrol to keep the price of ethanol lower. By 1994, 4.6m cars were powered totally by ethanol. The policy was relaxed in the 1990s and some cars again ran on petrol. In 2002 oil prices rose again and cars which could run on either fuel (flexible fuel cars) were developed. Ethanol is a clean fuel which helps to prevent greenhouse gases and is now exported to Sweden and Japan.

In addition to biofuels, Brazil is developing solar energy and has some large HEP schemes, such as the one at Itaipu on the Parana river, which have added to diversity of supply. However, lower river levels were allowed to develop which meant that electricity supply had to be rationed. Brazil has its own supplies of uranium and there are now two nuclear power stations at Angra.

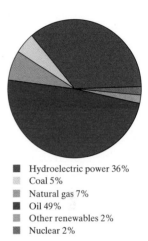

- Hydroelectric power 36%
- Coal 5%
- Natural gas 7%
- Oil 49%
- Other renewables 2%
- Nuclear 2%

Fig 6
Pie chart indicating Brazil's energy sources

Fig 7
The Itaipu Dam is a hydroelectric dam on the Parana River located on the border between Brazil and Paraguay

Brazil has found vast reserves of oil and gas in the Campos and Santos offshore basins. There are now networks of gas pipelines across Brazil, with the intention to link up to neighbouring countries. Coal reserves exist near Rio Grande de Sol, but it is poor quality steam coal and is used in power stations only.

Examiners' notes

You need to research energy supply in a contrasting location e.g. USA. Go to the US Energy Information website at www.ela.doe.gov.

Energy conservation

Energy conservation means reducing the amount of energy used. It can be done by greater efficiency and by using renewable resources.

The UK Sustainable Energy Strategy has plans for the use of more renewables, whilst improving the efficiency of energy from fossil fuels in energy production and transport. This will reduce pollution and waste.

Energy conservation initiatives include:

- Smart electricity meters installed in homes which allow people to see how much they are consuming in the hope that they will use less.
- High levels of insulation in new homes and the promotion of double and triple glazing and loft insulation schemes for older housing.
- Energy efficiency labels on washing machines to encourage the purchase of more efficient machines.
- Improving public transport systems, making them easier and cheaper to use. For example, in London, Oyster cards allow access to all forms of public transport. Initiatives also include developing more efficient and sustainable power sources for transport, e.g. using waste cooking oil to run buses and cars.
- More sustainable homes, which includes installing solar panels and ensuring efficient use of energy through high efficiency central heating boilers, lighting systems with low energy light bulbs and the landscaping and design of houses to maximize heat from the sun on the south-facing side.

Five 'eco-towns' have been proposed which will have their own renewable energy through solar panels and wind turbines and use district heating systems. The first one is being built at Hanham Hall near Bristol on a brownfield site. The first homes are due to be ready at the end of 2010.

Essential notes

In the UK, the Labour government set up a system, known as the Home Information Pack, to provide energy performance certificates that would give house buyers figures on energy efficiency and carbon performance. It would have exempted zero carbon homes from stamp duty and encouraged home owners to improve the energy efficiency of their homes. However, the coalition government abandoned this requirement for house sellers in 2010.

Essential notes

To follow the progress of the Hanham Hall development, go to: www.hanhamhall.co.uk

Fig 8
Hanham Hall is a planned 'eco-town'

Sustainable transport developments include:

- The development of light rail systems, e.g. the Manchester Metrolink from Altrincham to Bury, with a new spur to Media City, Salford, in 2010, and an extension to Chorlton by spring 2011.
- The congestion charge, which encourages the use of public transport in central London. The Greater London Low Emission Zone, introduced in February 2008, makes the most polluting vehicles pay a daily charge when they drive anywhere in Greater London.
- The development of **low carbon vehicles**. Car companies have marketed 'green' cars and fuel-efficient engines. The Toyota Prius was the first hybrid car but Nissan and Honda and other manufacturers are developing their own. Electric cars are becoming more reliable and can travel longer distances (up to 300 miles without recharging).

Fig 9
Manchester's Metrolink

Businesses can also be made more sustainable through promoting:

- Car sharing schemes
- Employees working from home
- New buildings with energy-efficient lighting and heating
- Carbon trading schemes

Marks and Spencer
The Plan A strategy includes energy-saving refrigeration system and aerodynamically designed fuel-saving transport. They were the first supermarket to encourage reuse of carrier bags by charging for new ones after May 2008. This has reduced the total number given out by 400 million per year.

Essential notes

Research the new goals for Marks and Spencer plan A at www.plana. marksandspencer.com

Global patterns of health, morbidity and mortality

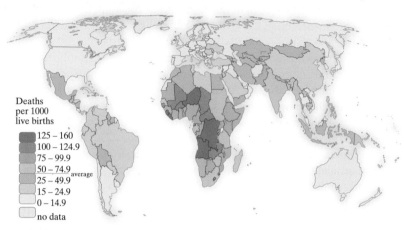

Fig 1
Global death rates per thousand population per year for 2006 (source, CIA world factsheet)

Deaths per 1000 live births

- 125 – 160
- 100 – 124.9
- 75 – 99.9
- 50 – 74.9 average
- 25 – 49.9
- 15 – 24.9
- 0 – 14.9
- no data

Crude death rate (CDR) is measured by the number of deaths per thousand people in one year. It is a measure of **mortality** (the death of people). The highest death rates are all found in the developing countries of sub-Saharan Africa except for Afghanistan. The highest of 21 per thousand or greater includes:

- South Africa, Botswana, Zimbabwe and Angola (the highest, with 23.04 per thousand) in the southern tropical and sub-tropical part of Africa
- Sierra Leone, Liberia and Niger in the tropical area of West Africa

A combination of factors can lead to countries having a high death rate. These could include infectious disease, climate change (and resulting famine), conflict and political repression.

The countries with the lowest CDR do not always correlate with the wealthiest countries. They include:

- The equatorial/tropical countries of Ecuador and Venezuela
- The sub-tropical countries of Mexico, Algeria, Libya, Saudi Arabia, and the Gulf states. The lowest is the United Arab Emirates with 2.08 per thousand.

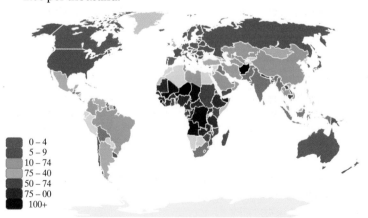

- 0 – 4
- 5 – 9
- 10 – 74
- 75 – 40
- 50 – 74
- 75 – 00
- 100+

Fig 2
Global infant mortality rates per thousand live births

Infant mortality rate (IMR) is an indication of the general health of a country. It is sensitive to changes in social and environmental conditions. It is measured as the number of deaths of children under the age of 1 year per thousand live births. The highest is Angola with 178.13 per thousand and the lowest is Monaco with 1.78 per thousand.

Morbidity refers to illness or disease, and the reporting of disease. Morbidity can be measured using the **disability-adjusted life year (DALY)**. This is a measure of overall disease burden, expressed as the number of years lost due to ill health, disability or early death. Originally developed by the **World Health Organization**, it extends the concept of potential years of life lost due to premature death to include equivalent years of 'healthy' life lost by virtue of being in states of poor health or disability. Some diseases have to be reported to the authorities. These include the most serious diseases such as cholera and yellow fever.

DALY for all causes per 100 000 population

- 60 000 – 83 000
- 40 000 – 59 999
- 25 000 – 39 999
- 19 000 – 24 999
- 14 000 – 18 999
- 0 – 13 999
- no data

Case-mortality rate (C-MR) is the number of people dying from a disease divided by the number who have that disease. E.g. UK in 2007 had 77 000 people diagnosed with HIV/AIDS and 500 deaths from HIV/AIDS. C-MR = 77 000/500 = 154. This means that 1 person out of every 154 infected with HIV/AIDS will die. In Zambia it is 1 person for every 19.64 sufferers.

Health in world affairs

Tackling the developing world's diseases has become a key feature of many nations' foreign policies over the last five years for a variety of reasons. Some nations see stopping the spread of HIV, tuberculosis (TB), malaria, avian influenza, and other major killers as a moral duty. Others see it as a form of public diplomacy, or as an investment in self-protection, given that microbes know no borders.

The World Health Organisation (WHO) is the directing and coordinating authority for health within the United Nations system. It is responsible for providing leadership on global health matters and monitoring and assessing health trends. One example of its work is the **Global Malaria Programme** (GMP). The World Health Organization employs experts to review evidence and set global policies regarding malaria. The GMP's policy advice provides the benchmark for national malaria programmes and multilateral funding agencies.

Examiners' notes

Investigate two countries, one with a high IMR and one with a low IMR. List factors that have led to their respective IMRs.

Examiners' notes

Once again prepare two case studies of countries at opposite ends of the DALY spectrum. To save time, try to use the same countries as opposite for all your case studies.

Fig 3
Age-standardized disability-adjusted life year (DALY) rates from all causes by country (per 100,000 inhabitants)

Essential notes

The WHO website (www.who.int/en/) is an invaluable source of information on health and disease. Use it to gather information about your chosen case studies.

Two case studies of diseases

Case study of an infectious disease

An **infectious disease** is one that can be transmitted from person to person or from organism to organism.

Malaria is an example of an infectious disease. About 3.3 billion people are **at risk** of contracting malaria.

Infection and spread

- Malaria is a **vector-borne disease**, the vector being the female anopheles mosquito. She passes the plasmodium (a parasite) from person to person.
- The female mosquito takes a blood meal from a human who already has malaria and takes in the plasmodium.
- It goes through the mosquito's gut and then arrives at the mosquito's salivary glands.
- She injects the parasites into a human's bloodstream when she feeds. These then move to the liver and reproduce in red blood cells. These eventually burst open.

The symptoms are: fever, sweating, cold shivering, malaise, enlarged liver, dehydration, organ failure, coma, fluid imbalance and brain damage. If it is not treated promptly it can lead to death.

Impacts: Malaria leads to about 250 million infections annually, and nearly one million deaths. 20% of all childhood deaths in Africa are due to malaria. It is estimated that an African child has on average between 1.6 and 5.4 episodes of malarial fever each year, with a child dying from malaria every 30 seconds. Pregnant women are at high risk not only of dying, but also of spontaneous abortion, premature delivery or stillbirth. Malaria is a cause of severe maternal anaemia and is responsible for about one third of preventable low birth-weight in babies. It contributes to the deaths of an estimated 10 000 pregnant women and up to 200 000 infants each year in Africa alone.

Malaria causes an average loss of 1.3% of annual economic growth in some countries. It traps communities in a downward spiral of poverty, disproportionately affecting poor people who cannot afford treatment and have limited access to healthcare. Malaria has lifelong effects by increasing poverty and impairing learning. It cuts attendance at schools and workplaces.

Treatment

Early and effective treatment of malaria can shorten the duration of the infection and prevent further complications. Unchecked use of **antimalarial drugs** in the past has contributed to widespread resistance of the malaria parasite to drugs such as chloroquine, leading to rising rates of sickness and death. Today, a new range of drugs is available known as **artemisinin-based therapies**. These have brought new hope in the fight against malaria.

The other way to control malaria is to control the mosquito. Long-lasting insecticidal nets can be used to provide protection to at-risk groups, especially young children and pregnant women. These are increasingly being distributed across Africa by governments and NGOs. The use of insecticidal sprays in the home is the most effective means of rapidly reducing mosquito density. Indoor spraying can be effective for 3 to 6 months.

Case study of a non-communicable disease (NCD): Coronary heart disease (CHD)

CHD refers to the failure of the blood supply to the heart muscle and surrounding tissue. It is the most common form of disease affecting the heart and an important cause of premature death in Europe, North and South America, Australia and New Zealand. CHD is known as a 'disease of affluence'.

Examiners' notes

Learn how to describe a global distribution from a world map such as this. Use reference points such as: tropical, equatorial, northern hemisphere, SE Asia etc. Note: naming individual countries does not give a clear description of distribution.

DALY for heart disease per 100 000 population

3000 – 5000
1800 – 2999
1200 – 1799
900 – 1199
600 – 899
0 – 599
no data

Fig 4
DALY for heart disease per 100 000 population

The effects of CHD

This can be measure in DALYs. CHD is responsible for 10% of DALYs lost in low and middle income countries and 18% in high income countries. It is increasing in developing countries and former communist states, partly as a result of increasing longevity, urbanization and lifestyle changes.

Heart and circulatory disease is the UK's biggest killer. In 2007, cardiovascular disease (CVD) caused 34% of deaths in the UK, and killed just over 193 000 people. Coronary heart disease, the main form of CVD, causes over 90 000 deaths a year in the UK: approximately one in five deaths in men and one in six deaths in women. It is a very costly disease. In 2003 CHD cost the UK healthcare system around £3 500 million.

Essential notes

Investigate one country that has a CHD problem. Make up a fact file that includes:

- The causes of CHD for the chosen country
- Trends
- Impacts on health
- Impacts on economic development
- Impacts on lifestyle

Food and health

Malnutrition

Malnutrition is the insufficient, excessive or imbalanced consumption of nutrients. A number of different dietary disorders may result, depending on which nutrients are under- or overabundant in the diet. The WHO cites malnutrition as the gravest single threat to the world's public health.

United Nations research has discovered that mortality due to malnutrition accounted for 58% of the total global mortality in 2006. In the world, approximately 62 million people die from all forms of malnutrition each year. One in 12 people worldwide is malnourished.

According to the WHO, malnutrition is by far the biggest contributor to child mortality, present in half of all cases. Underweight births and inter-uterine growth restrictions cause 2.2 million child deaths a year. Poor or non-existent breastfeeding causes another 1.4 million. Malnourished children grow up with worse health and lower educational achievements. Their own children also tend to be smaller. Malnutrition was previously seen as something that exacerbates the problems of diseases such as measles, pneumonia and diarrhoea. Malnutrition also causes diseases, and can be fatal in its own right.

Periodic famine

Famine contains three elements: food shortage, starvation and excess mortality. It has a greater effect on the most vulnerable in society. Famine is caused by many complex factors including: poor climatic and environmental conditions, population growth, market failure and war.

Obesity

Obesity is an increasing problem. The WHO predicts there will be 2.3 billion overweight adults in the world by 2015 and more than 700 million of them will be obese.

Impact on health: Experts are worried that the increase in obesity will lead to more health problems as people who are overweight have a higher risk of heart disease, Type II diabetes, and other diseases including some cancers.

Contrasting healthcare approaches

There are five different approaches to managing healthcare, depending on both the level of development of the country concerned and the political system concerned. These are:

- **Emergent:** e.g. India. Low government spending (<2% of GDP) with basic provision. Big differences between rural and urban areas.
- **Pluralistic:** e.g. the USA. Paid for by the consumer by insurance. Marginalizes the poor (44 million do not have private insurance cover – although President Obama modified this in 2010).
- **Insurance/social security:** e.g. France. Social security backed up by private finance. The patient pays for care, but then is largely reimbursed.
- **National Health Service:** e.g. the UK. Free at source, paid for by taxation. Prescriptions and some dentistry and ophthalmology paid for.
- **Socialized:** e.g. Cuba. 100% funded by the government.

Examiners' notes

Prepare a set of notes on one disease caused by malnutrition. Make sure you are able to describe its distribution and the effect that it has on the health of a population.

Essential notes

Ethiopia has had a series of famines, the last being in 2002. Investigate the reasons for the famine and describe the social and economic effects.

Essential notes

For one country, describe the effects of obesity on the nation's health. How might the problem be tackled?

Examiners' notes

Research two contrasting healthcare systems. Include: costs, funding, management, and effectiveness.

Health matters in a globalizing economy: transnational corporations

Globalization is defined by the UK government as: 'the growing interdependence and interconnectedness of the modern world through increased flows of goods, services, capital, people and information'. The growth of **transnational corporations (TNCs)** is one of the driving forces behind globalization.

Pharmaceutical TNCs

World trade in pharmaceutical products is huge. In Britain alone, pharmaceuticals brought in a trade surplus of £4.3bn in 2007. The value of UK pharmaceutical exports in 2007 was £14.6bn, more than £235 000 per employee.

Pharmaceutical TNCs have a variety of roles:

- **Producing a wide variety of drugs for sale:** These can either be **branded** (e.g. Neurofen) and relatively expensive, or **generic** (e.g. ibuprofen) which is chemically identical to the branded variety but much cheaper.
- **Producing essential drugs:** These are generic drugs that can provide safe and effective treatment for a variety of common but serious health complaints, e.g. diarrhoea. Essential drugs are mainly found in developing countries. The TNCs have tried to keep them out of their home markets.
- **Drug development:** This is the most expensive aspect of their business. Much of the research is directed towards developing drugs to control NCDs ('diseases of affluence'). This is because more money is made from them. Once developed, a patent is attached to the drug. Generic versions of the drug cannot be sold for 20 years.
- **Marketing and distribution:** A lot of investment is put into this. The TNCs target doctors, encouraging them to prescribe their drugs. Many of the branded, patented drugs are too expensive for developing countries to purchase, though sometimes deals are done to provide essential drugs cheaply (e.g. anti-retroviral medication for HIV/AIDS).

Tobacco TNCs and health

Smoking is responsible for a variety of life-threatening diseases. These include lung cancer, coronary heart disease, strokes and kidney failure. Most tobacco products are made by TNCs, though the Chinese tobacco market (with 300 million smokers) is state-owned.

With increasing pressure on sales in developed countries following extensive health education campaigns and legal changes (e.g. not smoking in public buildings), the tobacco TNCs have been targeting poorer countries. This has led to accusations that the tobacco TNCs have been aiming their advertising at children and women. The tobacco companies counter this charge by stating that they invest heavily in developing countries, improving wages and living conditions for all their workers.

Examiners' notes

Research one of the major pharmaceutical TNCs. Include in your research:

- The country of origin
- Locations of some of the R & D and manufacturing plants
- Their main products
- Any information concerning their role in improving health in developing countries

Essential notes

Go to the website of one of the leading tobacco TNCs and list the ways that they claim to be helping at least one developing country. It is always best to have both sides of an argument, even over tobacco.

Regional variations in health and morbidity in the UK

One measure that can be used to determine the health of a population is the **life expectancy** of that population. It is the expected (in the statistical sense) number of years of life remaining at a given age. Males and females are calculated separately.

Essential notes

When asked to describe regional variations, it is best to use the Government Office Regions of the Office for National Statistics. Less accurate, but just as acceptable, would be the use of counties or metropolitan counties. These all can be found at: www.statistics.gov. uk/geography/downloads/ uk_gor_cty1.pdf

Government Office Region	Male		Female	
	At birth	At age 65	At birth	At age 65
North East	76.4	16.7	80.6	19.3
North West	76.3	16.8	80.6	19.3
Yorkshire and the Humber	77.1	17.2	81.3	19.8
East Midlands	77.8	17.5	81.8	20.2
West Midlands	77.2	17.4	81.6	20.1
East of England	78.9	18.2	82.7	20.7
London	78.2	18.1	82.7	21.0
South East	79.2	18.4	83.0	21.0
South West	79.0	18.4	83.1	21.2
Wales	77.0	17.2	81.4	20.0
Scotland	75.0	16.3	79.9	18.9
Northern Ireland	76.4	17.0	81.3	19.8

Table 1
Life expectancy at birth and at age 65, United Kingdom, 2006–08

These figures show that people live longer (and are consequently healthier) in the South of England, and that the three other home countries have the lowest life expectancy. These figures hide more localized variations; Ceredigion in Wales has a male life expectancy at birth of 80.7, whereas the figure for Merthyr Tydfil is 74.9. In Scotland, the figure for Glasgow City is 70.7 but the figure for Edinburgh City is 76.5.

Mortality can also be considered by disease. **Table 2** shows the number of deaths attributed to coronary heart disease (CHD) for every thousand deaths of men and women under the age of 75. Note: These figures would be greatly enhanced if deaths of those over the age of 75 were added.

Essential notes

Investigate two of the Government Office Regions. Collect details of major causes of death and major disease morbidity. Add to this detail of at least two factors that might affect these figures (e.g. age structure, income and occupation type, education, environment and pollution).

Government Office Region	Male	Female
UK	65	21
North East	75	26
North West	76	26
Yorkshire and the Humber	70	22
East Midlands	63	20
West Midlands	69	20
East of England	53	14
London	64	20
South East	51	15
South West	52	15
Wales	69	23
Scotland	89	30
Northern Ireland	74	23

Table 2
Deaths attributed to CHD for every 1000 deaths of men and women under the age of 75

Death rates from CHD are highest in Scotland, and the North of England, lowest in the South of England, and intermediate in Wales and Northern Ireland. The **premature death rate** for men living in Scotland is 65% higher than in the South West of England and 112% higher for women. For more than 25 years these rates have been consistently highest in Scotland.

CHD morbidity

There has been a lot of research into regional morbidity of CHD. Geographic variations in CHD morbidity are not as clear as those for mortality. For example, although morbidity rates tend to be higher in the North than the South, higher rates also tend to be found in urban areas. Over 27% of the wards in London are in the top 20% of morbidity rates for men under 75 in England. This rises to 35% for wards in the North East, and is as low as 9% for wards in the South East. For women of all ages this range is even larger: 44% of wards in the North East are among the top 20% for female morbidity rates, compared to only 7% of wards in the South East.

There is also considerable variation within regions for CHD morbidity rates. For men of all ages, the rate for South Shropshire in the West Midlands is 624 per 100 000 whereas the equivalent rate in Wolverhampton is 1 216 per 100 000, nearly 95% higher.

Factors affecting regional variations in health

Age structure: In both Eastbourne and Worthing, on the south coast of England, 23% of the population is over 65 (6% more than the country average). Compare this with the London Borough of Wandsworth, where only 10% of the population is over 65. This difference is quite significant. The incidence of diseases of ageing (e.g. Alzheimer's disease) is more prevalent in these towns.

Income and occupation type: One example of how this can affect health is shown in **Table 3**.

Socioeconomic grouping of father	1 and 2	3, 4 and 5	6, 7 and 8	No father acknowledged
Birth weights less than 2500g (%)	4.5	5.6	8.2	9.5
Birth weights more than 3000g (%)	81.0	76.3	72.7	66.7

Education: The socioeconomic groupings are closely linked to education. Groups 1 and 2 are the wealthiest and the best educated as well as being the healthiest.

Environment and pollution: Results from studies carried out in Wales demonstrate the existence of some factor which increases the risk of childhood leukaemia at the edge of the Irish Sea. In view of the known association between leukaemia and exposure to radiation it seems possible that exposure to radioisotopes released from BNFL Sellafield and subsequently brought ashore along the coast of Wales is the most likely explanation.

Essential notes

In the UK the Office for National Statistics uses the following socioeconomic groupings:

1. Higher managerial and professional occupations
2. Lower managerial and professional occupations
3. Intermediate occupations (clerical, sales, service)
4. Small employers and own account workers
5. Lower supervisory and technical occupations
6. Semi-routine occupations
7. Routine occupations
8. Never worked and long-term unemployed

Table 3
Birth weights correlated to socioeconomic grouping of father

Local healthcare provision

Since its launch in 1948, the NHS has grown to become the world's largest publicly funded health service. With the exception of charges for some prescriptions and optical and dental services, the NHS remains free at the point of use for anyone who is resident in the UK. It covers everything from antenatal screening and routine treatments for coughs and colds to open heart surgery, accident-and-emergency treatment and end-of-life care.

The number of patients using the NHS is huge. On average, it deals with 1 million patients every 36 hours. Each week, 700 000 people will visit an NHS dentist, while a further 3 000 will have a heart operation. Each GP in the nation's 10 000-plus practices sees an average of 140 patients a week.

The NHS provides a range of services. These include:

- Hospitals
- Emergency and urgent care
- Dental services
- GP services
- Eye care services
- Pharmacies
- Mental health services
- Social care

These are augmented by the private sector. For example, within the dentistry sector the rapid growth in private dentists reflects both the demand for services not otherwise available through the NHS (such as teeth whitening) and the lack of availability of NHS treatment itself. Private practice is attractive to dentists in areas where the growth of incomes has enabled patients to afford to pay for a more personal service.

Factors that affect the provision of healthcare facilities are:

- **Age:** Those areas dominated by youthful populations have a greater need for services such as: antenatal clinics, maternity hospitals, obstetrics, health visitors, paediatrics and sexual health clinics. A structure dominated by older people will require: care/nursing homes, elderly mentally ill services (EMI), respite care and health visitors.
- **Gender:** Populations in which there is a greater proportion of females will have greater need for services such as breast and cervical cancer screening. For more men there will be a greater need for coronary health clinics and testicular cancer screening.
- **Wealth:** In deprived areas there will be a greater need for much more localized services, including GP and NHS dental surgeries, health and diet education services, advice to quit smoking and alcohol/drug abuse rehabilitation centres. Populations of wealthier areas generally have access to health and fitness centres. They may choose to opt out of the NHS provision and use private facilities.

Examiners' notes

The specification states that candidates must complete a local case study of healthcare provision. Choose an area you are familiar with. Use the 2001 census returns at www.ons.gov.uk/census/get-data/data-sources/index.html to get background information on the population of your chosen area. Use the local primary case trust website to research available services.

Local case study of healthcare provision

It is possible to use the census data from the Office for National Statistics (ONS) to gather information about the health of a population at a local level. **Table 4** shows selected details of two wards in St Helens, Merseyside. Rainford is a dormitory settlement on the urban/rural fringe and Parr is an inner urban area previously dominated by manufacturing and coal mining.

Factors possibly affecting health provision	Rainford	Parr
Total population	8344	12082
Male/female (%)	48.4/51.6	48/52
Social grade 1 & 2 (%)	7	1
Unemployed/never worked (%)	1.4	6.4
Age 65+ (%)	19.9	17
Age < 16 years (%)	20.1	22.6
General health good (%)	67	57.8
General health not good (%)	9.92	16.8
Long term illness (%)	21	29.0

Table 4
Factors possibly affecting health provision in Rainford and Parr, St Helens

It can be inferred from the data that Rainford is the wealthier of the two wards, has an older population and has better health.

Both wards fall under the jurisdiction of the St Helens and Halton **Primary Care Trust**. The hospital provision is managed by St Helens and Knowsley NHS Hospital Trust. There are two main hospitals in St Helens, both close to Parr. Through NHS 'Choices' people in Rainford may opt to go out of the PCT, to a nearer provision at Ormskirk.

Rainford has two dental surgeries and an orthodontist. Of the two dentists one is private and the other only partly NHS. Parr has only one dental surgery (NHS), but its proximity to the town centre means that dental care can be accessed there. Rainford has two GP practices, Parr only has one. Rainford has an optician and a pharmacy, Parr has no opticians and two pharmacies. Parr has much better provision for exercise than Rainford. There are a variety of council-owned and private gyms all within a 2 km radius. Rainford has none.

The main determining factor between the varying provisions appears to be the wealth difference. This is reinforced by the fact that Rainford is 6 km from St Helens town centre, whereas Parr is only 1.5 km away. More people in Rainford are able to travel to chosen, often private, health facilities, whereas the less wealthy people of Parr use local NHS and local authority services.

AQA Unit 1 GEOG 1: Physical and human geography

This unit is tested by a two-hour examination. It consists of two sections, A and B. Section A comprises the physical core and three physical options; section B comprises the human core and three human options. You must attempt both core questions and one option from each section.

Each question is made up of:

- Short, **point-marked** questions worth 4 marks or fewer. These are point marked (i.e. each relevant correct statement is awarded 1 mark).
- Structured questions. These are awarded marks based on the **level** of quality of the answer.
- Extended prose questions. These are worth 15 marks and are, again, marked based on the level of quality of the response. There are three levels for these questions.
- Below you will find sample questions followed by (tinted boxes) containing the comments and advice of examiners. You will also find sample answers; the examiners have commented on these.

Rivers, floods and management

Rivers, floods and management is the core Physical section and all candidates must study this section.

Part (a)

Briefly describe the ways in which a river transports its load. [**4 marks**]

The examiners are looking for four separate points here. Simply naming the processes of transportation is not enough; each one has to be explained for a mark. Thus: *'traction is a form of river transport'* will only be credited if it goes on to say *'this is when stones are rolled along the bed of the river'*.

Average answer

A river transports its load in four ways. The first process is traction where rocks and larger material are rolled along the bed by the river. Pebbles and other similarly sized material are transported by saltation, which bounces material. Suspension is the process by which sand particles are transported by the rivers carrying them along. Solution, the last process, is the transportation of dissolved material by the river.

The description of suspension is not clear and so this would be allocated 3 marks.

Strong answer

There are four main methods of transportation in rivers. The first is traction. During this process large particles, such as cobbles or boulders are rolled along the channel bed by the force of the water. In addition to this, saltation is used, whereby slightly smaller debris is effectively bounced along the river bed. These terms are collectively known as the river's bedload. Thirdly, suspension, the most common method of transportation, involves smaller particles such as clay and silt being carried while suspended in the river. The final method is solution, in which sediment is dissolved within the mass of water.

The maximum mark of 4 is given for this answer.

Part (b)

Using figure 1 describe the relationship between mean flow velocity and particle size for the process of erosion.
[4 marks]

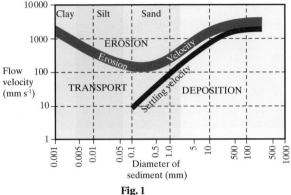

Fig. 1

This question requires you to understand not only the general ideas behind the Hjulstrom curve, but also to be able to understand the significance of the logarithmic scales. Remember, each cycle of the scale increases by a factor of 10. On this type of scale, 5 is more than two thirds of the way between 1 and 10. Like all questions requiring you to read graphs, you should be looking for things like maximum, minimum, trends and anomalies. It is important also to realize that for this question you are only to describe the erosion curve.

Average answer

Generally, the larger the size of load (also known as the calibre) the greater velocity that is required to erode it. **Too vague for a mark yet.** However, there are exceptions, mainly the need for a higher velocity to erode smaller clay particles. This is because they often converge into larger masses that require turbulent flow to enable them to be entrained. **This explanation is irrelevant.** The Hjulstrom curve above indicates how a river of a low velocity, such as 10 cumecs, cannot erode any material while a faster-flowing river of 100 cumecs can erode large clay, silt, sand and gravel particles but cannot erode higher calibre particles.

The candidate has also incorrectly interpreted the vertical scale but credit was deserved for stating that the higher the number (on the vertical axis) the coarser the named material could be eroded. 2 marks.

Strong answer

The critical erosion curve outlines the relationship between velocity and load size. The smallest material, clays and silts, require a greater velocity to erode them; e.g. clay needs around 100cm/sec to erode it due to electrical bonding and an adhesive quality. **This explanation is irrelevant.** As load size increases the velocity needed to erode it decreases. This is principally the case for sand particles. Then, as particle size increases, velocity needed to erode also increases, with pebbles, for example, requiring 100 cm/sec at least to erode.

The response has correctly identified the relationship between load size and correctly identified velocities. The shape of the entrainment velocity curve is described. 4 marks.

Part (c)

Figure 2 shows a landform resulting from fluvial action. Describe this landform and explain its formation. **[7 marks]**

The two command words are 'describe' and 'explain'. In order to achieve the higher marks you must:

*   Refer to figure 2, clearly describing the meander in the photograph and not just a generic meander
*   Clearly explain how this meander has been formed
*   Make sure that there is a balance between the description and the explanation.

Fig. 2

Average answer

The landform in the photograph is a meander. This is a sharp bend in a river. They usually occur in the middle and lower stages of a river. Meanders are formed from pools and riffles. The helicoidal flow of the river means that the thalweg hits the outside of a river bend. Then, by a process of hydraulic action and abrasion, it undercuts the bank and makes a river cliff. On the inside of the bend, where the flow of water is slower, pebbles and sand are deposited to form a point bar. Over time meanders migrate to form a flood plain.

Apart from the opening statement the answer does not refer to the photograph. The whole answer is a generic description of meanders and so cannot get into Level 2. The use of the correct terminology in the explanation would be creditworthy if the terms were defined in some way. Discussion about the future is irrelevant and in this case, incorrect. Level 1: 3 marks.

Strong answer

This is a meander. I can tell this because it is a sharp bend in a river with a steep bank called a river cliff on the outside of the bend and a beach of pebbles called a point bar on the inside of the bend. The examiner can tell that the photograph is being referred to here. The river cliff has some clumps of grass at its base which shows that the bank has collapsed recently. Meanders are formed because rivers rarely flow in a straight line for long. Where there is a bend in the river the fastest flow of water goes on the outside of the bend because of centrifugal force. This water undercuts the bank by the process of hydraulic action, using the weight of the moving water. This is an unclear explanation of the process. This process is most effective when the river floods because it has greater velocity and so more kinetic energy to carry out erosion. The clay banks will slump down, but the top of the slump will be held together by the grass roots. Eventually the slumped soil will be washed away and the process starts again. The slowest water is on the inside of the bend. Here the water is so slow that it cannot carry the pebbles and so these are deposited.

This response clearly describes the photograph. There is a balance between the description and explanation. The explanation is not complete and few geographical terms are used. However, there are two processes clearly linked to the landform and both are expanded upon and developed. Level 2 awarded: 7 marks.

Part (d)

Rejuvenation is responsible for the formation of several landforms. Describe these landforms and explain how they were formed. **[15 marks]**

The extended prose mark scheme uses three level descriptors:

- In **Level 1** the student describes at least one landform, and/or begins to explain how the landform is created. Equally, the student may concentrate on one landform only, or concentrate only on either description or explanation. Waterfalls which are not linked to rejuvenation can only reach maximum marks within Level 1.
- In **Level 2** there is specific description of at least two landforms, the explanation is more focused, and there is a balance between description and explanation.
- In **Level 3** there is a clear description of landforms and the landscape. Links to processes are clearly made and the student is able to show that there are different types of the same landform (such as different forms of terraces, meanders).

Average answer

Rejuvenation is the process whereby a river is given more erosive power in the form of potential energy due to a drop in the river's base level. The point at which this occurs is often indicated by a sudden drop in the channel bed known as a knickpoint. This often results in waterfalls, as the increased erosive power allows a river to erode at a quicker rate down through layers of hard rock that overlie soft rock, leading to an overhang. The increased velocity of the water as it flows over the overhang leads to undercutting through erosion of the soft rock. Eventually the hard rock cap may collapse due to a lack of support and the debris is then used to rapidly abrade the surrounding rock by the turbulent flow of the water, forming a plunge pool. An example of this is the High Force waterfall in Upper Teesdale, the tallest waterfall in the UK. This process may then continue, causing the waterfall to retreat upstream forming a steep-sided gorge.

Despite a reference to a relevant landform – knickpoint – early in the answer, much of this is generic waterfall formation and does not necessarily apply to rejuvenation.

Another landform that occurs as a result of rejuvenation is an incised meander, such as the one at Durham ☞

in the northeast of England. When rejuvenation occurs, originating meanders can gain more potential energy, which is used for increased vertical erosive power. The channel bed of the meander can be deepened leaving an incised meander with steep cliff-like banks.

The other main landform associated with rejuvenation is terraced floodplains, which are, essentially, floodplains at different elevations that occur on top of one another, leading to different layers of flat land. Here, an increase in erosive power causes a sudden drop in the channel bed as the river erodes downwards. A new floodplain is created on the river's new level of flow through lateral erosion and the deposition of its load following flooding. These floodplain terraces can often be identified in alternating steps of flat elevated land.

This answer starts with a generic explanation of a waterfall, with only a tenuous link to rejuvenation. Balance is added by the inclusion of incised meanders and river terraces. This brings in a second and third relevant landform and some appropriate though incomplete explanation. The answer would have benefited from some diagrams, indicating to the examiner that the candidate knows precisely what a rejuvenated landscape looks like. Mid-Level 2 awarded: 9 marks.

Strong answer

Knickpoints are formed due to rejuvenation, as they show where the old long profile meets the new long profile. They are formed when the river is rejuvenating and trying to adjust to the new base level. Knickpoints may be small landforms or they may cause waterfalls due to the steep change in gradient. River terraces are also landforms resulting from rejuvenation. They are former floodplains which are left high above the level of the river. This is because, as the river rejuvenates, it cuts deeper into the ground and therefore a new floodplain is formed, leaving the old floodplain (river terrace) above the level of the new one. Incised meanders are also landforms resulting from rejuvenation. There are two types of incised meander, ingrown and entrenched. Ingrown meanders occur when the meander keeps its meandering course but erodes vertically as it adjusts to the new base level. Ingrown meanders are ☞

asymmetrical in shape, with a steep river cliff and shallower slip-off slope. Ingrown meanders are caused where the vertical erosion is quite slow. Entrenched meanders occur when vertical erosion is faster, meaning that the meanders are more symmetrical in shape. They are very deep and have steep sides. Entrenched meanders are also caused due to the river keeping its meandering course, but have increased vertical erosion due to rejuvenation.

> The answer covers the full range of landforms (knickpoints, river terraces, incised meanders, ingrown meanders) created by river rejuvenation. There is a balance between description and explanation, especially in the case of the incised meanders. Although there is not a clear definition of rejuvenation, the answer clearly shows an understanding of the formation of a rejuvenated landscape. Top Level 3 awarded: 15 marks.

Cold environments

Part (a)
Explain what is meant by 'periglacial'. **[2 marks]**

> This question would be point-marked. The examiner is looking for a brief definition with a spatial element.

Average answer
Periglacial is an area with permafrost and a temperature below freezing for most of the year apart from in the summer when it slightly rises above freezing.

> Only a partial description is given in this answer. 1 mark.

Strong answer
Periglacial environments are areas on the edge of glacial environments where the temperature fluctuates around 0°C, causing freezing and melting in the active layer.

> This answer would score 2 marks – there is a clear definition with location of areas. The term 'active layer' is used in the correct context.

Part (b)

In the context of glaciers, explain what is meant by the process of abrasion. [**2 marks**]

This question would be point-marked. The examiner is looking for a brief explanation of the process using the correct terms.

Average answer

This is when the glacier begins to pick up material which it uses to scrape at the bedrock and wear it away.

This answer is very brief but does show an understanding of the term. 1 mark.

Strong answer

Abrasion occurs when rocks and stones embedded in the ice as en-glacial moraine work their way to the bottom of the ice where they are in contact with the bedrock. They are then dragged along by ice movement wearing away the bedrock to form a smooth surface. They often leave long scratches called striations.

Clear and detailed answer using correct terms. 2 marks.

Part (c)

Give reasons for seasonal changes in the active layer. [**4 marks**]

This question would be point-marked. An understanding of the meaning of the term 'active layer', along with reasons for seasonal variation and use of correct terms, would be expected.

Average answer

The active layer freezes in the winter; however, in the warmer seasons it melts to form a non-frozen active layer of 1–2 metres. Solifluction then occurs as a slope of even 2° can cause the saturated active layer to move as it cannot infiltrate the ground due to the ice. This solifluction process results in solifluction lobes as the ground slopes down.

This answer needs to give a definition of the term 'active layer' and explain the difference between different surfaces on the rate of refreezing, e.g. lakes and vegetation cover. The candidate also needs to explain that permafrost is impermeable. Information about solifluction is not relevant for this question. 2 marks.

Strong answer

In the spring the insolation warms the active layer causing it to melt whereas in the winter, periglacial areas receive less sunlight, become colder, and therefore the water in the active layer refreezes. When it melts the following spring, the water in the soil again melts from the top downwards; the frozen subsoil stops water infiltrating into it and allows the soil to start to move even on the most gentle of slopes.

This answer has not defined the active layer although the answer shows some understanding. There is an attempt at an explanation of the seasonal changes but the answer needs more detail, preferably including statistics. 3 marks.

Part (d)

Describe and explain the formation of one of the following landforms: pingo, arête, or drumlin.
[7 marks]

Make sure you choose only one, not all three! This is a common mistake made by students. Note that the marks are for description of the feature (shape, size; what it looks like) and also for an explanation involving processes.

This answer is level-marked:

- **Level 1** requires a general description of the landform's shape and/or the beginning of an explanation of how it was formed. Some use of appropriate terms.
- **Level 2** demands a detailed description and clear explanation. Alternative explanations may be suggested. Appropriate geographical terms are used.

Average answer

Drumlins. A drumlin is an oval-shaped mound caused by a glacier. When the glacier slows down it drops some of the material it is carrying, smoothing it over and continuing down the valley with the steeper side facing up valley. This is a glacial depositional feature found in lowland areas where glaciers are moving more slowly. It produces a hummocky landscape. Sometimes several drumlins are found together as a basket of eggs landscape.

This student clearly has some knowledge of drumlins and describes the landform with some accuracy using some correct terms, gaining a good Level 1 mark, but the answer is not clear or precise enough to reach Level 2. 4 marks.

Strong answer

Drumlins. A drumlin is a glacial deposition feature. As a glacier loses velocity, for instance as it enters a lowland area or picks up more debris or even begins to melt, it cannot carry its load, so it starts to leave some of the material it is carrying behind as a mound of unsorted glacial till. As soon as it has dropped some of its load it is able to speed up again and carry more material so it smoothes over the remaining material forming an oval-shaped mound with the steeper end facing up valley and the smoother side down valley. These features are often up to 50 m in height and 1000 m long. They often form in swarms, creating an undulating landscape known as basket of eggs topography, as seen in Northern Ireland around Strangford Lough.

This student has written a precise answer with actual dimensions, examples and correct terminology. Two explanations for the loss of velocity are given although more detail could be added. However, this answer would still achieve a good Level 2. 6 marks.

Part (e)

Cold environments are fragile environments. Discuss the sustainability of developments in ONE such area you have studied. **[15 marks]**

Examiners are looking for one clear case study, with a clear definition of sustainable development. The best answers should be balanced between development and conservation, together with considering short-term and long-term effects. The answer should cover environmental, political and economic aspects of development in the chosen area and should end in a conclusion that answers the question, putting the student's own view backed up by evidence from the previous paragraphs.

In an answer requiring some discussion, QWC (quality of written communication) can enhance the examiners' understanding of answers and enable you to make points clearly and concisely, raising marks. Poor QWC can interrupt the flow of the argument or discussion and limit the marks. On the front of each examination paper it states:

'You will be marked on your ability to: ☞

- Use good English
- Organize information clearly
- Use specialist vocabulary where appropriate'

Make sure that you show your ability to do this, especially in the 15-mark questions.

There are three levels to the mark scheme:

- **Level 1** will be awarded for description of some developments and or conservation schemes. Points made are basic.
- **Level 2** will be awarded where description is more accurate and uses correct terms. The answer may make links between conservation and development. There are references to sustainability. Some balance in the answer. Some evidence to support points made.
- **Level 3** is for a clear, well-organized discussion that answers the question. Specific examples and evidence are quoted to support answers and links are made between ideas. Clear references to sustainability. The answer is balanced and a logical conclusion is drawn based on the evidence given.

Average answer

Antarctica has a very fragile ecosystem due to its harsh climate. Say more about the climate and why this is a fragile environment. Any developments must be sustainable. Need to define this term. In 1968, 12 countries signed up to a treaty which helped preserve the ecosystem. Need to give details. As tourism could generate lots of capital it must be developed. However, Antarctica must be protected too. Subsequently, no tourism more than 100 people is allowed on shore at any one time at any one place. This means that animals and ecosystems are not disturbed too much. Also, cruise ships are not allowed to discard oil or waste in the seas nearby. This balance allows money to be made from tourism but prevents the ecosystem being damaged. Now a clear idea of development and sustainability balance.

There is also an abundance of oil in Antarctica. However, as it is not needed at the moment it is important that it is not exploited due to the damage it will do to the environment. Needs to say what the damage ☞

might be. In 1998 the Madrid Protocol put a ban on oil extraction for 50 years. This has prevented over-development of the fragile area, meaning it is protected. Another piece of evidence for protection of the area. Clear Level 2 now. Also, in the 1950s and 1960s, the area was being overfished and whaling caused the whale population to decrease to below 100. Quotas have subsequently been put in place preventing too much fishing. This allows the area to be developed due to the large amount of fishing but also protects the area from being overfished. Due to the extremely low numbers of whales, however, there has been a complete ban on whaling unless used for scientific research. Again some evidence given at Level 2 but links are not clear. Explanation of short Antarctic food chain would be useful here. Next sentence does not follow from this statement.

This means the area can continue to develop as a hub of scientific research in tundra area- Note this is incorrect. while the whale populations recover and become protected. ☞

This answer needs a conclusion in answer to the question. Overall, it is a sound answer but needs to develop points more fully and with more specific ☞

details. It also needs to develop more of an argument or discussion. This answer would reach a mid-Level 2. 10 marks.

Strong answer

Antarctica *Identifies an appropriate area straight away.* is a fragile environment due to its cold average temperature of −49°C and harsh climate, which means few species can survive and adaptation is slow, and it relies on keystone species in its food webs such as krill. Its intrinsic value as a place of great beauty and the last surviving wilderness untouched by humans, make it very special and it must therefore be protected. However, the continent has many valuable resources and uses which there is great pressure to exploit. These developments need to be carefully monitored to ensure that they are sustainable and do least harm to this environment in the future. *Good introduction mentioning specific facts – temperatures, krill, and explaining why it is a fragile environment, plus a definition of sustainable.*

Antarctica has great fuel and mineral reserves, including 10% of the world's remaining coal reserves, over 10bn barrels of oil and huge reserves of iron ore under the Trans-Antarctic Mountains. The Madrid Protocol of 1998 struck a balance between protecting the continent from development and allowing exploitation of these resources – which may cause noise and pollution damaging to birds which live in the area. The Protocol conceded that due to the depletion of reserves in the rest of the world and the increasing demand for resources, the mineral resources may one day have to be exploited. The Protocol is due for review in 2048. *Economic aspects covered using specific evidence which is relevant to the question and discussion of balance between development and protection. Could have mentioned specific birds or looked at ☞*

effects on penguin colonies. Long-term issues and developments discussed. A Level 2 answer now.

The current tourist industry has a good balance between development in the region and protection of it. The International Association of Antarctic Tour Operators applies regulations such as allowing no more than 100 people on land at once, and ensures there are briefings on appropriate conduct before leaving the boat while allowing income to be generated by tourism. All waste generated has to be removed in order for this area to remain a wilderness. *Tourism development is discussed and a balance between protection and development is highlighted. Specific evidence is given. Level 2.*

The Convention for the Conservation of Antarctic Marine Living Resources strikes a good balance between exploiting fish stocks by allowing fishing but setting quotas, e.g. a 2.75m-tonne limit on annual krill catches. However, more still needs to be done to prevent illegal fishing, particularly of the Patagonian toothfish, of which 2600 tonnes are illegally caught each year, such that the species is seriously threatened. *Again, specific evidence given on environmental and economic aspects. Level 3 now.*

Antarctica can be developed sustainably, but international agreements, such as the Madrid Protocol, will have to be kept if mining operations in particular are not to damage this last wilderness.

A logical conclusion based on specific evidence, linked together to answer the question. A balanced, succinct answer at Level 3. 15 marks.

Coastal environments

Part (a)
Describe the characteristics of destructive waves.
[2 marks]

Average answer
The waves have a small crest which means they are not very high or powerful. They collapse as they reach the beach and have very little energy. The frequency of destructive waves is 10–12 per minute.

The bulk of this answer is about constructive waves, which is thus incorrect in this context, and therefore gains no marks. The candidate is rescued by their last sentence, which is correct and would gain 1 mark.

Strong answer
The waves are relatively short in proportion with their height and have a weak swash but a strong backwash. They are high energy destructive waves that deposit material.

This answer mentions height, wavelength, swash and backwash. It could also have mentioned frequency, but still does enough to gain 2 marks.

Part (b)
Describe the effects of destructive waves **[3 marks]**

This question would be point-marked. It is always a good idea to read the questions ahead of the one you are answering. This question asks about effects whereas the previous one asked for a description of the waves. Make sure this doesn't catch you out.

Average answer
Destructive waves help to wear away beaches as they have a strong backwash which removes material from the beaches. Destructive waves create offshore bars.

Effects are correct but this answer is a little brief and more detail is needed. 2 marks.

Strong answer
Destructive waves have a strong backwash and a weak swash which means sediment is removed from the beach, which is steep. Deposition creates a bar out to sea from the material removed. Beach cusps often develop from the strong backwash. Destructive waves usually occur in storm conditions and at high tide, and may throw material up onto the back of the beach forming a storm beach.

A full answer which gains the maximum. 3 marks.

Part (c)
How does sub-aerial weathering affect the erosion of the coast? **[4 marks]**

This question is point-marked. The examiners are looking for an answer which explains how sub-aerial weathering adds to marine processes.

Average answer
Sub-aerial weathering is where the cliffs and coast are eroded by non-marine erosion. This can include chemical weathering, such as acid rain, or biological weathering, which is caused by plant and tree roots breaking through the soil as well as burrowing animals. This also includes freeze-thaw weathering. Sub-aerial weathering erodes away the top of the cliff, weakening it while the sea erodes the base.

This answer needs to explain how this process helps the coast to erode and has not made the links clearly enough. It does offer some explanation of sub-aerial weathering processes though, which is worthy of credit: 2 marks.

Strong answer
Sub-aerial processes of weathering, including biological, chemical and freeze-thaw weathering, help to break up the structure of cliffs that are exposed even at high tide. They break off sections of rock from the main structure or alter the general structure of the coastline. Material is then free to be removed by mass movement, causing the retreat of the coastline. These processes speed up cliff retreat as more than just marine processes are affecting the cliffs and the tops of the cliffs are being affected.

This answers the question and mentions the correct terms in context. It would have been better if the types of weathering mentioned had been explained in some detail: 3 marks.

Part (d)
Explain the formation of stacks. **[6 marks]**

The examiner is looking for a concise answer which explains the sequence of events resulting in a stack. A relevant example would improve the answer, as would explanation of the relevant processes. In this question there is no requirement to draw a diagram or sketch. If you do prefer to add a diagram to help your explanation, ensure you refer to it in the text of your answer, because the examiner would read the text first and then look at the diagram to see if it gave any extra information or made a point clearer.

This answer would be level-marked as shown below:

- A **Level 1** answer would have a basic explanation with some correct terms. There may be gaps in the sequence of formation.
- For **Level 2**, the explanation is clear with the full sequence explained, including processes. Appropriate terms are used.

Average answer

Areas of coastline have headlands of hard rock where waves erode cracks and joints in the rock. This makes the rock retreat leaving a wave-cut platform and a cliff. This is not relevant to stacks. Stacks are islands just offshore, formed when an arch collapses, e.g. Durdle Door in Dorset. This is because the waves break under the roof of the arch at high tide and weakens it. Stacks which get further eroded are called stumps.

This answer is basic with a correct location and part of the sequence, but no discussion of processes and some irrelevant information (regarding wave-cut platforms and stumps) which gained no further marks. A basic answer at Level 1: 2 marks.

Strong answer

Differential erosion occurs where the cracks and joints occur in bands of otherwise hard rock. These weaker areas are eroded away by marine processes and sub-aerial weathering. Hydraulic action, where the pressure of the water is forced into cracks by the waves, forces the crack to open, eventually becoming a cave. Abrasion, using the sand and pebbles dashed at rocks by the waves, wears away the inside of the cave until it becomes larger. These processes are especially active on headlands where waves are concentrated. Where two caves meet back to back on a headland the back wall collapses forming an arch. The waves continue to batter the underside of the arch until the roof collapses leaving a stack as a separate island, e.g. Old Harry, Dorset.

This is a full answer. It could have included reference to the start as a geo and explained the importance of solution of limestone, but it still gets the maximum 6 marks.

Part (e)

With reference to case studies, evaluate the success of coastal management using soft engineering. **[15 marks]**

This question requires specific reference to case studies – which means two or more. The command word 'evaluate' needs addressing in a conclusion which should state whether the evidence in your answer suggests that soft engineering is a success or not.

This question is level-marked as follows:

- At **Level 1**, the student describes one or two soft engineering management strategies. General points or location only are mentioned. Points made are basic and not linked together.
- At **Level 2**, description is related to specific locations and there is discussion of relative success (or cost benefit analysis) and a discussion of issues of coastal management.
- **Level 3** is awarded with a clear evaluation of different schemes. There is a logical discussion of various schemes and together with a judgement about their relative success.

Average answer

Black Water estuary in Essex has used soft engineering management. Areas of land have been allowed to flood and sea defences have been breached. Soft engineering is more sustainable compared to hard engineering. However, it has social, economic and environmental issues.

Good start with clear case study example. It needs to explain why soft engineering is more sustainable.

Allowing land to flood reduces the use of land. That land could be used to build on and provide space for housing or industry. This has an economic impact as it restricts the amount of growth of areas (e.g. places surrounding Essex could grow and extend but can't because the land has been flooded).

This is very vague. It needs to make a point about use of cost-benefit analysis.

Potential or old farming land has been destroyed, which again prevents economic growth as that land could have been used to grow crops or rear cattle which would have contributed to the economy. This also affects farmers' livelihoods, as, if their land is flooded ☞

and destroyed, they will have lost their income and home.

Still vague – the student needs to explain how the flooding of this land might protect other areas which have greater economic use or where lives are at risk.

The land that has been flooded will have destroyed habitats for animals and would have killed many species living there – this may lead to extinction. Land will now be too salty to grow crops on; only plants that can grow in high salt levels will survive, e.g. sea lavender.

This continues to be vague and is not entirely correct. New habitats are created as new salt marsh develops. Salt marshes can be used as pasture for grazing sheep. The answer is confined to only one case study and would benefit from others, e.g. where sand dunes at the coast have been managed to protect the land behind, such as in The Netherlands.

This answer shows some understanding of the basic ideas, with one location and one real issue discussed. Ideas are not linked into a full discussion of costs and benefits and other schemes are not mentioned. The answer is a little brief and only just gets to Level 2: 7 marks.

Strong answer

Along the Holderness coast severe coastal erosion occurs due to the unconsolidated boulder clay. At Spurn Head soft engineering strategies have been adopted. Soft engineering aims to work with natural processes and to manipulate and maintain natural structures to defend against erosion without altering their fundamental structure.

Good definition but needs examples of strategies.

At Spurn Head managed retreat is being used as the land is of low economic value and therefore as a result of cost benefit analysis isn't viable for hard engineering protection. By allowing some erosion a greater supply of sediment will result that will help with the dune regeneration so that the psammosere environment can be maintained, which may help reduce the effects of coastal erosion.

A relevant idea but need to explain how this works in more detail. ☞

Also in Essex the soft engineering strategy of coastal realignment and salt marsh creation is being adopted. The Abbott Hall Farm project aims to reduce coastal squeeze by removing the protective wall and allowing pioneer plants to colonize the mudflats to create a protective salt marsh. This scheme will save £500 000 that would have been spent on building hard engineering structures, and it therefore has economic benefits.

A second example with specific details, moving the answer to Level 2, but would be better with a full explanation of coastal realignment and explanation of how the mudflats help to prevent erosion further along the coast.

Also, the scheme is welcomed in Europe, as halosere environments are rare in Europe. The Abbotts Hall Farm project is showcasing the benefits of soft engineering, as money and a fragile habitat are being saved while protecting the stretch of coastline from erosion. Many types of wildlife, particularly birds, will also benefit ☞

from the scheme. However, soft engineering projects often take longer to become established (e.g. dune regeneration and marsh creation) and so their effects may not be felt instantly after they are adopted.

Some details of wildlife would have helped, though the timescale introduced here is useful. ☞

This response needs a conclusion to argue whether these projects are successful in order to answer the question. Some relevant points are made and two case studies are used with some specific evidence. A high Level 2 answer: 12 marks.

Hot desert environments and their margins

Part (a)
What are the differences between arid and semi-arid areas? [2 marks]

The differences between arid and semi-arid are so clear that you have to have the exact numbers to gain any credit. The amount of precipitation received by an area is the most straightforward way of tackling this question, although the use of a named aridity index would be equally valid.

Strong answer
An arid area is one that receives less than 250 mm of rain a year and a semi-arid area is an area receiving between 250 and 500 mm of rain a year.

There is credit for the climatic definitions based on precipitation. 2 marks.

Strong answer
Arid areas have less than 250 mm of rainfall per year whereas semi-arid have between 250 and 500 mm of rainfall per year. Generally, the temperatures in the arid areas are also higher than the semi-arid areas.

This gains 2 marks for the comments about the rainfall amounts. The statement about the temperatures would not get credit, but in this case it is not needed to get the maximum available.

Part (b) (i)
Figure 1 shows vegetation in Death Valley, California, an arid area. Describe the main characteristics of the vegetation shown in the photograph. [3 marks]

The key to this question is to describe **what can be seen in the photograph**. Any statements about reduction of water loss, dew collection and competition are all irrelevant here. The photo shows that the plants are spread out, with thin, woody branches and small spiky green leaves. There appears to be a lot of dead material near the base as well as some exposed roots.

Fig 1

Average answer

The vegetation has a small leaf surface allowing as little water lost to evapotranspiration. Irrelevant point In addition it has very thin stems which show it is not a water storage plant like a cactus. From looking at the bush I would presume it is a water-seeking plant due to it appearing to cover a larger area than other plants found in the desert.

> The last statement is not clear enough to credit the plants being spread widely apart. 2 marks.

Strong answer

This vegetation appears to be xerophytic and has developed characteristics to make it drought resistant. For example, the plant has small leaves that will reduce the potential water loss occurring, This point is irrelevant. and has many thin branches that will increase the amount of dew the plant collects. The plants are spread far apart so that they are not competing with the other plants. Again, this is irrelevant.

> Despite irrelevant explanation, the description is good. 3 marks.

Part (b) (ii)

Explain how the vegetation of arid areas is adapted to the climate. **[4 marks]**

Once again this is a point-marked question. The focus of this question is on an explanation of how the plant adaptations enable vegetation to survive in dry places. There are no marks for the description of the vegetation, but it is necessary to include some description so that the adaptations can be explained. You may refer back to the photograph, but it is not necessary. An example of a relevant point would be to state how plants are able to reduce transpiration.

Average answer

There are water storage succulents like cacti which have minimum leaves and rubbery surfaces to prevent transevaporation. Some plants are only seasonal ephemerals – these only germinate and flower during or after rainy periods. Other plants take up large surface areas, close to the ground where it is cooler, and tap down deep into the soil to find water. ☞

There is credit for the statement about 'minimum leaves' which examiners took to mean few leaves. Then there is credit for the rubbery surfaced cacti, the ephemerals and the plants that tap deep into the ground, so 3 marks are given here. Note that although the candidate misnames transpiration, the examiner is able to see what the candidate intended.

Strong answer

Vegetation in the desert has adapted to either avoid droughts, become drought resistant, or store water. Drought avoidance plants germinate flowers and seed within two weeks of rain, and have thin, tough rubbery skin and rough bark which reduces evapotranspiration. Water storage plants store water in their stems or roots, like cacti; water-seeking plants, like the creosote bush, have long ☞

roots which control the water source of a wide area.

Credit is initially given to the list of adaptations. A list comprises of two or more named adaptations without any further detail. There is then credit for each of the ways that vegetation (in the list) adapts to the aridity. This answer could have gained 5 marks but has reached the maximum available of 4 marks.

Part (c)

Describe the different sources of water in hot desert environments. Explain how these sources contribute to water in hot deserts. **[6 marks]**

There are three sources of rivers in deserts (exogenous, ephemeral and endoreic). There is also artesian water, coastal fog, dew and rainfall.

The mark scheme comprises 2 levels:

- A **Level 1** answer describes sources of water in the desert. There is also some simple explanation of how the water gets to the desert. To get the upper end of this level there should be appropriate geographical terminology present.
- For **Level 2**, the description of water sources is more precise. The answer indicates that the candidate is clearly aware of two (or more) sources of water in arid regions. There is a clear explanation of how the water can be at that source. Appropriate geographical terminology is used throughout.

Average answer

One type of source found in the desert is endoreic streams. These rise outside the desert, often in mountains, and flow and end in the desert. Another source of water is exogenous streams such as the Nile and the Colorado river. These rise outside the desert and flow continually and end externally. Ephemeral streams form when there is heavy rainfall and are formed and end in the desert – they often only ☞

survive for a few weeks.

There are also oases and water holes which form when water flows through impermeable rock and rises to the surface in the desert.

This account describes four sources of water in the desert, but the descriptions are not precise. In the case of the oases, it is incorrect. There is only a weak attempt at explanation. Level 1: 3 marks.

Strong answer

One source of water is from exogenous streams, where a stream begins within the reaches of a mountain and continuously flows through a desert, for example the Nile. Another source of water is rainfall, although this occurs scarcely. When it does there are often torrential downpours which cannot be infiltrated so run as ephemeral streams through the desert which dry up after the rain event. Oases are another form of water source in hot deserts as water stored in impermeable rock strata near the surface of the ground and the surface may be removed by deflation. It causes the ☞

aquifer to be near the surface and become available to plants and animals. Dew, which forms in the cold temperatures at night, can be used as a source of water by many plants and animals.

> The description of the sources of water is precise, particularly the ephemeral stream description. There are four sources of water described and there is clear explanation, especially of the oasis water. The use of terms such as ephemeral and deflation show that the candidate uses the appropriate geographical terminology. 6 marks.

Part (d)

Assess the sustainability of different strategies used to manage land use in contrasting arid areas of the world. Your answer must include agricultural strategies.
[15 marks]

The main command word in this question is 'assess'. To gain higher level marks you must have detailed case studies of land use management and be able to say how sustainable those strategies are. This means that you have to be able to produce evidence of their sustainability.

This is an extended prose question and so is marked in three levels. They are:

- In **Level 1**, the candidate describes some strategies but only in a limited way. The answer may concentrate on one case study only, or be unbalanced between case studies. Points made are simple, ☞

random and/or generic and not linked to the named area.

- For **Level 2**, the description of management strategies is more specific. Two contrasting areas have been clearly referred to and there is some evidence to support statements about sustainability. There may be some reference of agriculture in the context of land use. The answers may be imbalanced to one of the named areas. The assessment of the level of sustainability is limited.

- At **Level 3**, there is a clear description of management strategies in at least two contrasting arid (or semi-arid) areas. There is good support using detailed case studies. It is an organized account that responds quite clearly to the question with the sustainability aspect as a main focus. There may be a balance between agriculture and other land uses. The candidate has made clear statements assessing the level of sustainability of management in at least two contrasting areas.

Average answer

Sustainability is making sure that the management method is long-lasting but isn't a detriment to the natural environment.

In Burkina Faso, which is situated in the Sahel, they have set up a scheme called stone lines, where stones are put in areas of fertile soil and seeds are also planted, so that when it rains the water collects and stays in this area. This therefore grows food for the people. The advantages of this scheme is that it uses natural ☞

materials from the environment so they will not run out, but the negatives are that the food shortage requires immediate help whereas this scheme takes a very long time so therefore isn't as sustainable for the people living in the Sahel.

In Southern Spain, which is an MEDC, there is a shortage of water in certain places like Murcia and Andalucia, therefore the hydrological plan has been introduced which tries to move the water from areas which have a lot of water to areas which are ☞

sparse in water. Also on the plan is the desalination of water so that water is not wasted and can be reused. However, the downsides to this plan are that it is only short-term and desertification is still occurring and desalination will cost around 1.2 billion. In conclusion, there are schemes that are offered which do improve the lifestyle of the population but none of the ☞

schemes is sustainable for the future.

> There are two contrasting areas, Spain and Sahel, and there is some limited support. There is reference to agriculture in the Sahel, but there is little detail, and the assessment of sustainability is tentative. This answer just reaches Level 2. 8 marks.

Strong answer

The Sahel is an area of land made of nine countries, all with very arid climates. They are also some of the poorest and most deprived countries in the world. It is the home to millions of people and as a result resources like firewood, water and food are in very short supply. Crops are the main sort of food but lack of water, good soil and powerful wind means food is both poor quality and scarce. One area named, but no strategies are given so far – simply a list of difficulties and general background.

The main way in which this problem has been attempted to be tackled is through the use of stone contour lines. These walls both block the wind and trap moisture in the form of dew, meaning the little precipitation available is used sparingly. Organizations have helped tackle this problem and they have also tried to encourage the planting of trees and other plants to encourage a better ecosystem and better soil quality. They have also given the people solar cookers to try and limit their use of fuel wood for this reason as well as a lack of resources.

A range of strategies is given here. ☞

Alternatively, in America, a much more developed and wealthy country, they have erected dams. The dam known as the Hoover dam controls the reservoir of water in the Colorado river. This is used as drinking water as well as for hydroelectricity in order to allow for the development of large settlements like Las Vegas. The dam has allowed for this development within Las Vegas to take place. This incredibly expensive means of controlling the sustainability of life in Las Vegas is a total contrast to the cheap and resourceful methods used by the people of the Sahel.

> An alternative area is given, again with some statements of strategies. The answer shows an awareness of contrasts. It refers to both the Sahel and the USA with some support. However, references to sustainability are implicit. This was awarded mid-Level 2. 10 marks.

Population change

Population Change is the core Human section and all candidates must study this section.

Part (a)
Outline the factors influencing life expectancy.
[4 marks]

The command word 'outline' here indicates that a brief description of the factors is needed. This answer would be point-marked.

Weak answer

The factors influencing life expectancy are that people live longer. There are lots more older people living into their 90s now and many living to over 100. This causes lots of problems for developed countries because they have to support older people from taxes paid by the working population. This has caused many countries to raise the state pension age, from 60 to 62 in France, and in the UK there are plans to raise it from 65 to 66 years.

This answer is not relevant to the question. The student has explained the effects of increased life expectancy, but has not considered the factors which have led to longer life – the causes of short or long life expectancy– so does not gain any marks.

Strong answer

In developing countries life expectancy is as low as 48 (in Niger), because there is little access to healthcare, resulting in high infant mortality rates and earlier death. In developed countries life expectancy is longer with many people living into their 90s because of improved healthcare, better nutrition and good sanitation and hygiene. Health and safety at work and a good standard of living combined with good education all help to increase life expectancy. War in any part of the world will obviously lower life expectancy.

This is a clear answer directly relevant to the question. It has discussed longer and shorter life expectancy and given a number of relevant factors. It could be more specific in places, and have given more examples, but it would still achieve the full 4 marks.

Part (b)

Describe and explain the shape of a population pyramid for a country which has experienced in-migration. **[4 marks]**

This answer would be point-marked. It does not ask for an illustration, so there are no extra marks for this, but a sketch might help the explanation.

Average answer

Countries which have in-migration will have a bulge in their pyramids where the migrants have arrived. This bulge is around the 20 to 30 age group, especially on the male side.

This answer is a correct description but the question also asks for an explanation so only achieves 2 marks.

Strong answer

The population pyramid will show an increase in the 20 to 30 age group by a bulge at this point on the pyramid. Most migrants are economic migrants and it is still young men who are especially likely to move to another country to find work so the bulge will be larger on the male side. Many migrants return to their home country when they have earned enough money so the pyramid returns to its original shape. Women are now joining this migration for work and so pyramids will again show a bulge in the 20 to 30 age group but in some countries this will show as a bulge on the female side as well.

The population pyramid has been described and the reasons explained so this answer would achieve full marks. It would have been even better if an example had been quoted. 4 marks.

Part (c)

Explain the limitations of the Demographic Transition Model. **[7 marks]**

This question would be level-marked as follows:

- At **Level 1**, the answer shows clear understanding of the DTM but is mainly a description of the DTM.
- At **Level 2**, the answer not only explains the DTM but also explains the limits of this theory – for instance, in having to extend it to include a stage 5.

Average answer

The DTM starts with birth and death rates high. This means that population does not grow. It then shows the death rate declining but the birth rate does not fall until stage 3, which is where there is most growth. In stage 4 the birth rate and death rates are equal so there is no growth. The limitations of the DTM are that it shows what happened in the past and it doesn't give reasons for the changes.

This answer is mainly descriptive and this is not detailed. The limitations are only basic so it does not reach Level 2: 3 marks.

Strong answer

The Demographic Transition Model (DTM) reflects the changes in the population of the UK from the time of the Industrial Revolution to the present day. It compares birth and death rates and shows the changes in growth as being in four stages. Stage 1 is where the birth and death rates are high and cancel each other out, by stage 2 the death rate falls and there is fast growth and birth rate remains high. In stage 3 the birth rate falls and by stage 4 birth and death rates are both low so the rate of increase is very low as well. The DTM was a model which showed changes over a long period of time in what is now a developed country. Modern medicine and healthcare have decreased the death rates in many countries very quickly and so the process is much faster in developing countries which do not follow the model. Perhaps the biggest change is in developed countries where the death rate has become lower than the birth rate leading to a decrease in population, e.g. in Hungary, and the model did not take account of this so it has had to be adapted by adding a stage 5. It may have to be changed again in the future.

This answer examines two limitations with reasoning for one of them. The second limitation has an example (Hungary) but the reasons are not fully explained. 6 marks.

Part (d)

Referring to case studies, evaluate the success of policies adopted by governments in an attempt to manage birth rates. **[15 marks]**

This question needs actual case studies. Ensure that only policies to regulate birth rates are discussed and that policies are included which have the effect of both increasing and decreasing the birth rate. ☞

The question also asks for an evaluation so you will be expected to write a conclusion based on the evidence you give, which will say whether or not these policies have been successful.

This question is level-marked:

- A **Level 1** answer gives a basic description of a policy or policies, which is mainly descriptive with no or little evidence of links to real case studies. There are isolated facts which are not linked together. Evaluation is not present or basic.
- A **Level 2** answer has a clear description of policy/policies and relevant case study/studies ☞

are used. There may be an attempt at explanation of the need and/or effects of policy together with an attempt to justify. The answer may include reference to policies which both increase and decrease birth rates. Evaluation is implicit.

- A **Level 3** answer is thorough, detailed, well written and well organised. Several different policies are discussed, which may include policies which increase and decrease birth rates. Strong evidence from case studies is used as support. Evaluation is explicit.

Average answer

Governments try to manage birth rates in order to control the dependency ratio. This is the number of people who are working to support a young or older population who are not working. If there are not enough working and too many young people then taxes will have to rise to pay for education and healthcare for the young. *Attempts to explain the need for policy but still only at Level 1.*

If a country has too many young people they may want to persuade people to have fewer children. They can do this through encouraging the use of contraception and sterilization programmes so that fewer children are born. The law on abortion was changed in some ☞

countries which has also had an impact on the birth rate. *Several different policies mentioned, but none developed or related to case studies.*

Other policies include encouraging migration so that there are fewer people to use resources, and encouraging people to work longer to provide for the increasing number of young people. *This is not relevant to controlling birth rates.*

I think governments should control birth rates because otherwise there will be too many people for the country to support.

This last point is personal opinion and not supported by evidence so the answer stays at Level 1: 5 marks.

Strong answer

Countries sometimes need to reduce their population and try policies such as family planning programmes to help reduce the birth rate. In many countries this is a voluntary programme which is made easily available and free such as in the UK. The UK has a low birth rate anyway but countries such as India also tried to encourage people to use contraception by putting clinics into rural areas and a big advertising campaign encouraging people to have only two children. The campaign did have some success but the population ☞

is still growing and there were accusations of enforced sterilizations at one stage where some states tried to reduce the birth rate more quickly. *A good opening paragraph with a case study and evaluation.*

In China the one child policy was strictly enforced and their population was reduced considerably through a drastic fall in the birth rate. The country was accused of severe measures including the 'granny police' who informed on anyone who was likely to break this policy and allowing late abortions to enforce this policy. ☞

Another good example of a relevant case study and policy. Answer is now at Level 2.

In Singapore economic measures helped to reduce birth rates through increased taxation on larger families and voluntary sterilization was rewarded by a paid holiday and improved housing and schooling for the family. This policy was successful in lowering the birth rate. In fact it could be argued that it had been too successful as the birth rate is now too low. A further example of birth rate reduction at Level 2. However, with correct data to support it (e.g. birth rates were lowered from 29.5/1000 in 1965 to 17/1000 in 1987 or other relevant facts) this would have raised the answer to a higher point within Level 2.

In conclusion, there are several government policies to manage population and they all seem to have been successful in meeting their targets to some extent. ☞

Some have however caused other long-term problems such as in China where there is now a shortage of females due to the one child policy whereby male children were preferred.

A coherent conclusion based on evidence with several policies and case studies but does not discuss policies to increase birth rates. This is a good Level 2 answer, and gains 11 marks. In order to access Level 3 the student needed to include some of the following: policies which may increase birth rate; more factual evidence with statistics; an explanation of the need for population policies that both reduce and increase birth rates; an explanation of the effects of policies in more detail with some clear statements of success or otherwise.

Food supply issues

Part (a)

What is meant by 'the geopolitics of food'? [**4 marks**]

This question is point-marked. There is an internal maximum mark of 3 imposed for answers that only concentrate on either a definition of geopolitics, or information about the politics of food.

Strong answer

Geopolitics of food is the politics which happen between different areas whether it is globally or not. It is where countries try to sell and buy food and protect their own farmers. The two main components of geopolitics is free trade and food security. To try and get the best results by using things such as tariffs, quotas and subsidies, exporting and importing food.

One mark is for the general comment about countries protecting their own farmers. The second is for the list of the two main components, free trade and food security. Another mark is for the list of methods that could be used, tariffs and quotas. 3 marks.

Strong answer

This relates to how governments globally deal with goods via imports, exports and growing/producing. This includes things such as tariffs and 'dumping' and how countries globally interact with each other through imports, exports, producing and tariffs.

There is a mark for the general definition. This is then reinforced by the comment on imports and exports. There is a further mark for the examples of controlling trade, tariffs and dumping. The final clause is repetition. 3 marks.

Part (b)

Outline the characteristics of an extensive livestock farming system. [5 marks]

The mark scheme is divided into two levels:

- In **Level 1**, the candidate describes features of either an extensive farming system and/or ☞

livestock system of agriculture. The answer is made up of unconnected simple statements.
- In **Level 2**, the candidate describes features relating to the combination of extensive and livestock farming systems. A wide range of characteristics clearly linked to this farming system is given.

Average answer

This is pastoral farming so animal rearing. As it is extensive this means low inputs of capital and labour put in over a large area of land. The output can be relatively low. An example would be cattle rearing. You breed animals either for subsistence or commercial, you do not use intensive methods such as hormones or large capital investment. You feed the animals and allow them to grow at their own pace.

This response gains Level 1 credit for stating that there are low inputs over a large area, with a relatively low output. It lacks detail of either location or of why the system would be followed. Although there is some incorrect material in the answer the candidate is not penalized. This is awarded Level 1: 3 marks.

Strong answer

An extensive farming system is one that usually takes up a lot of land. The livestock refers to animals such as cattle, sheep or goats. Usually, for farmers to choose this way of farming, there is a lot of land available and the grazing is not very good. This means animals have to move a lot to get enough grass. One place that uses this system is in Australia. Here there are huge cattle stations as big as Wales. There are only a few people to manage all this area. The grazing is poor because it is on the edge of the desert and often suffers drought.

This response recognizes that a lot of land is involved and gives reasons for farmers choosing to work extensively. There is an example quoted and there is some detail of that example; this reassures the examiner that the candidate fully understands the terms. Top Level 2: 5 marks.

Part (c)

Study the extract below, from a Fair Trade publication about cocoa (chocolate) production.

The cocoa industry

It is estimated that there are approximately 14 million people directly involved in cocoa production. Globally, 3 billion kilograms of cocoa were produced in the 99/00 harvest season.

Farmers get barely 5% of the profit from chocolate, whereas trading organisations and the chocolate industry receive about 70%.

A 1998 report from UNICEF stated that some Ivory Coast farmers use child slaves, many from poor neighbouring countries such as Mali, Burkina Faso, Benin and Togo. It is estimated that some 15,000 children between the ☞

ages of 9 and 12 have been sold into forced labour on cotton, coffee and cocoa plantations in northern Ivory Coast in recent years.

West African economies are critically dependent on cocoa. Cocoa revenues account for more than 33% of Ghana's total export earnings and 40% of the Ivory Coast's total export earnings.

90% of the world's cocoa is grown on small family farms of 12 acres or less.

Fluctuating prices on the world commodity markets give cocoa producers a precarious existence. The flourishing child slavery trade in Ivory Coast is partly a result of cocoa producers being desperate for cheap labour to work on the plantations. On the New York Coffee, Sugar and Cocoa Exchange, cocoa prices dropped from a high of $US1,800 per tonne in 1997 to $US982 in 2001.

Using the extract and your own knowledge, explain the problems faced by cash crop producers in developing countries. **[6 marks]**

The mark scheme for this has two levels:

- At **Level 1**, the answer describes the problems faced by cash crop producers but does not explain why they have arisen; there is a heavy reliance on the extract and little evidence ☞

of a wider knowledge.

- At **Level 2**, the candidate uses both the information in the extract as well as her or his own knowledge. There is explanation of why the problems described in the extract and elsewhere are such an issue. To get to the top of Level 2 there must be evidence of wider knowledge about cash crop production.

Average answer

Cash crop producers face many problems. The cocoa growers only get 5% of the profits from the sale of chocolate and that is unfair and only just enough to live on. The rich countries buy the chocolate at cheap prices and sell at high prices maximizing their profit. The farmers need very cheap labour and so in some places like Ivory Coast they are using child slaves. The changing prices in cocoa and other cash crops make it difficult for the farmer to make plans for the future.

The response has used the information from the extract well. A link has been made between the unfair trade and the increase in slave labour. Unfortunately there is not much use of the candidate's own knowledge and so this answer is confined to Level 1: 4 marks.

Strong answer

Growing cash crops means that farmers have to compete against bigger corporations that can sell their cash crop cheaply, this means that the smaller farmers have to lower their costs. This means that some of them use slave labour to save money. Another problem of growing cash crops in LEDCs is that they use up valuable land which means that traditional crops can't be grown. This can lead to food price rises while the value of the cash crop falls like the chocolate price.

The answer makes use of the extract and there is some of the candidate's own knowledge added to it. The response also makes a link between the candidate's own knowledge to that given in the extract (i.e. local food price rises while chocolate prices fall). Level 2: 5 marks.

Part (d)

Discuss how food supply and demand can be managed in two contrasting ways. **[15 marks]**

The mark scheme for the extended prose question has three levels:

- At **Level 1**, the candidate describes at least one approach to managing food supply and/or demand. Points made are simple and there is no attempt at comparison.
- At **Level 2**, the answer begins to consider the advantages and/or disadvantages of more ☞

than one approach to managing either supply or demand. The candidate may start to discuss more than one approach. There is tentative commentary as these approaches are discussed. Statements can be supported by some case study detail.

- At **Level 3**, there is a clear summary of approaches to both supply and demand. Advantages and disadvantages of both supply and demand control systems are made clear and there is support given throughout. The candidate makes detailed comments about the systems.

Average answer

Two approaches of managing food supply and demand are the Green Revolution and genetic modification. ☞

The Green Revolution was to produce food more efficiently. The Green Revolution consisted of a HYV being made which was a seed that was drought resistant and ☞

could absorb more nitrogen from the soil thus improving the size of the yield. Advantage. It first benefited India. This is incorrect. which used the HYV seed that produced cereals such as maize. This increased the yields of the crop. They increased the usage of fertilizers and irrigation.

Genetic modification of food is an approach to manage food supply and demand because it is suggested that it could solve food shortages in the future. The USA and China are largely involved in this scheme. An example of genetic modification would be of the rice in China where rice is a staple food for over two thirds of the world but to grow rice is not efficient as it uses a lot of water and is very vulnerable to drought but the new ☞

genetic modification of it makes it more resistant and more of it can be grown. This means more can be grown for the increasing demand of it. The Green Revolution was supposed to improve productivity in many countries such as the Philippines. In India, the Green Revolution caused problems as it increased debt for small farms, increased the use of fertilizers while GM crops reduce the input of fertilizers.

> The two approaches (Green Revolution and GM crops) are addressed but they are not clearly contrasting. They are both concentrated on the supply side, with little emphasis on demand. The answer lacks balance and detail, though it does have some merit. Low level 2: 7 marks.

Strong answer

The Common Agricultural Policy (CAP) reform aimed to get rid of the surplus which was formed from the original CAP. They tried to do this by enforcing quotas on some products such as milk. A big policy which CAP reform put forward was the need to look after the environment for future generations and make it sustainable. One way in which they encouraged this was the stewardship scheme where farmers were paid money to care for the land with things such as set-aside, limits on hedge cutting and creating habitats for animals. Another scheme was for farmers to diversify away from large scale farming into things like B&Bs and holiday homes. This generated more income and also reduced the amount of produce. Note: these are not CAP policies.

This worked well in reducing the surplus and sustaining the environment for the future and reducing fertilizer use which became excessive in the original CAP era which led to eutrophication in streams and other environmental damage. Advantages.

Another approach is the Green Revolution which was set up after the Bengal Incorrect. famine in the 40s. This encouraged land expansion, double cropping to produce more food and high yielding seed varieties. Although this worked and is still widely done in India, many problems have occurred such as vast eutrophication due to excessive fertilizer use, babies born with deformities due to excessive pesticide use, richer farmers benefit more ☞

as they can afford the high yielding seeds, the long term health effects of the high yielding seeds are unknown and MEDCs and TNCs are hugely benefiting as they are the ones who sell the seed and determine the prices.

Food demand can be managed by changing consumers' minds about what they want to eat. One way that this has been done is shown by the rising demand for fair trade goods. This is because there has been a lot of work done by fair trade organizations to get supermarkets to adopt their goods. The Co-operative Society has done this in a big way and sells all sorts of fair trade items including chocolate and coffee.

On a much bigger scale, the big supermarket chains like Tesco can use their purchasing power to demand that farmers supply what they want, at the prices they want. The supermarkets are constantly monitoring their customers' demands with loyalty cards and so can make the farmers produce what customers want. There is now a balance between approaches to managing food.

> There are two approaches (the CAP and the Green Revolution) to do with supply, with some support. There are also two approaches to the demand side of the question. There are clear links to food supply in the section on the Green Revolution, and clear links to demand in the comments about Tesco. There is some comment on their effectiveness. Top level 2 is awarded: 12 marks.

Energy issues

Part (a)
Comment on the distribution of oil reserves worldwide.
[4 marks]

This question would be point-marked. Note that it asks for a comment which requires some observation beyond just description, which may be reasoning. To describe a distribution means you need to describe a pattern. Make use of the map provided.

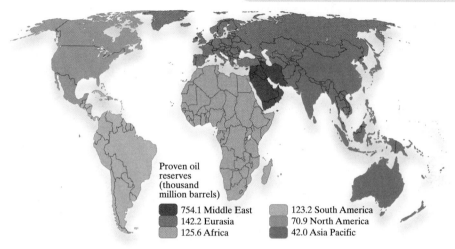

Proven oil reserves (thousand million barrels)

- 754.1 Middle East
- 142.2 Eurasia
- 125.6 Africa
- 123.2 South America
- 70.9 North America
- 42.0 Asia Pacific

Fig. 1

Figure 1 above shows world proven oil reserves.

Average answer
The global distribution of oil is that oil is mainly in the Middle East in places like Iraq. The oil is also found in the USA, Canada, Alaska, Russia, Indonesia and the Gulf of Mexico and the North Sea. There are some new finds in Brazil. There are reserves in Antarctica, but these will be difficult to exploit.

This answer is very brief and consists of a list of places where oil has been found. Some are countries and some are regions and they are not presented in a logical order. There is no explicit reference to the map. An overall pattern with some idea of the amount of oil available is needed plus some more details on reserves and possibly a comment on the cost of exploration or geopolitics. Needs more details. 2 marks.

Strong answer
Oil reserves are only exploited where oil exists naturally in large amounts. The biggest fields are in the Middle East, especially in Saudi Arabia, and this oil is relatively easy to mine. Other high-yielding fields are found in Eurasia, especially Russia. The USA, in Alaska and the Gulf of Mexico, also has good reserves, but these 👉

are more costly to mine due to climatic factors (the extreme cold in Alaska and the depth of the reserves under the sea bed in the Gulf of Mexico.) Exploitation depends on demand and the costs of production and although the costs are high in these last locations they are in the USA which has a high demand and large market so it is worth exploiting here despite the 👉

high costs of production. The high demand means that these reserves are used up more quickly.

It also means a secure oil link as the Middle East oil is in a politically unstable area. There are some resources in Europe in the North Sea and large finds now in Indonesia and Brazil. There are new reserves in the Russian Arctic which again are expensive to mine but will be nearer the market. ☞

This answer has details about areas of the world which have the larger reserves and makes some use of the map. There is an understanding of the costs of production in more difficult areas and the relative speed of use of reserves. There is a brief discussion of geopolitics and proximity to markets which acts as a comment. This answer would score the full 4 marks.

Part (b)

Explain the causes and effects of acid rain. **[6 marks]**

This question asks for causes *and* effects, and expects reasons to be given. Case studies should be given if possible. It is level-marked:

- A **Level 1** answer gives a basic account of the

causes and/or effects of acid rain. There may be brief reference to examples.

- A **Level 2** answer gives a more detailed explanatory account of both causes and effects, with clear reference to case studies and using the correct terminology.

Average answer

Acid rain is caused by sulphur dioxide from power stations making the rain acidic. The winds take the clouds from the UK and it rains over Germany. Germany lost a lot of tree growth and forests died and fish died in the acidic lakes. They said it was because of our power stations burning fossil fuels especially coal. We now use low sulphur fuels like gas and Germany have added lime to the soil and lakes to counteract this acidity so things are much better now.

This is a brief and basic answer with one clear cause and brief effects in a given location, but nothing is explained or developed enough. There could have been mention of other gases involved, the nature of the prevailing winds. Material on solutions is not relevant to the question. 3 marks.

Strong answer

The causes of acid rain are that rain is slightly acidic anyway. Rainwater takes in carbon dioxide from the atmosphere and becomes a weak solution of carbonic acid. When fossil fuels are burnt not only do they add to the carbon dioxide, but also to the production of sulphur dioxide and in the case of cars, nitrous oxides as well. These make the rainfall even more acidic. In some places, like Haverton Hill near Billingham, in the 1950s, the rain was as acidic as pH 4 as it came from the nearby factories. Its effects were to strip paintwork off buildings and put holes in artificial fibres like nylon.

This rain also caused the trees to stop growing properly and the crowns of the trees lost leaves. It also caused fish to die in lakes and rivers, which also became acidic. The effects were noticed in Sweden and Germany and they alleged that it was coal-fired power stations in the UK which caused the pollution as the SW prevailing winds brought acid rain from the direction of the UK towards these areas.

This answer has explained both causes and effects in some detail and mentioned particular areas affected so gains the full 6 marks.

Part (c)
How can homes be designed for energy conservation?
[5 marks]

This is level-marked:

- A **Level 1** answer briefly describes some energy conservation measures.
- A **Level 2** answer explains each point fully, giving examples of where energy conservation has been tried and how it works to help conserve energy.

Average answer

Homes can be designed for energy conservation by having double glazing and an efficient boiler and insulation. They should buy energy efficient light bulbs and save water by reusing dirty water and not running the tap when cleaning your teeth. *Some of this section is about water saving rather than energy conservation.* Also not using your car for short journeys and having a more fuel efficient engine. Homes should try to recycle everything including bottles and plastics. *Again, this is not relevant to the question.*

This answer is very basic and has moved away from the point of the question so it gains only a mark within Level 1: 2 marks.

Strong answer

Modern housing is built with energy conservation in mind. Insulation is thick to reduce heat losses and windows are double-glazed. There are grants for the elderly in the UK to improve their housing insulation. Smart meters can be installed and energy-efficient boilers, washing machines and other goods are fitted into new builds. Some housing projects are installing solar panels. As long ago as 1972 Milton Keynes were building solar houses to provide solar heating for hot water systems. Larkfleet is one of a number of new home builders who build and design sustainable housing. In Oakham they have built a sustainability house which has features such as rainwater harvesting, solar panels, energy-efficient boilers and smart metering.

This answer started well and attempts to explain how some of the methods help conservation of energy. It has referred to a specific project, and a house builder, but there should be more explanation of how the other ideas might help to conserve energy. It is a Level 2 answer and would score 4 marks.

Part (d)

Discuss the advantages and disadvantages of nuclear power in providing energy for the future.
[15 marks]

This question asks for a discussion and will expect a conclusion at the end based on the evidence in the answer. You will need to ensure a balance between advantages and disadvantages, and explain how you think it might help/not help to provide enough power in the future.
This answer is level-marked: ☞

- A **Level 1** answer describes the advantages and/or disadvantages of nuclear power in a simple way.
- A **Level 2** answer begins to discuss the relative advantages and disadvantages in a more detailed way. There are some case studies as evidence. The answer stays at this level if it is not balanced.
- A **Level 3** answer is thorough, detailed, well written and well organized. There is discussion of several advantages and disadvantages. Good evidence from case studies is used as support. A conclusion is drawn based on the evidence.

Average answer

Nuclear power is a controversial form of power. Some people think it is not safe to live near a nuclear power station because of the risk to health as there have been cases of leukaemia allegedly linked to areas near nuclear power stations. Needs more balance in the introduction.

The nuclear power stations produce radioactive waste which has to be disposed of. This can be done on the site of the power station by sealing it in steel canisters and burying it deep underground. However, it remains radioactive for thousands of years and that means that future generations will have to look after it and ensure that nobody comes to any harm.

New nuclear power stations will also have to be built. While most can be on the site of an existing reactor there will be protests at any new sites because many people are not happy living near a nuclear power station. This would have been improved with an example.

Nuclear waste also has to be transported to be reprocessed and this causes worries over accidents. After Chernobyl people did not trust nuclear power and the government decided to run down these power stations in the UK. This means that if the UK wants to use nuclear power in the future they will have to ☞

build new power stations. These are very expensive to build and take a long time. Many argue that nuclear power is not cheap because you have to build in the high maintenance and safety costs and the cost of decommissioning when the power station has finished its useful life. The reactor core remains and has to be buried in concrete. A lot of disadvantages are given here. Examiners would be waiting for an advantage to provide balance in the answer.

Uranium has to be imported and will eventually run out so nuclear power is not a renewable power source.

Present sites for nuclear power stations are at the coast. Many people feel that they spoil the view and some are worried about the environmental impact along the coast in case of an accidental spillage. Again this would have been improved with one or more examples.

In conclusion, although nuclear power produces a lot of power I do not think we should rely on it for the future.

This is a very brief conclusion. The answer in terms of disadvantages is clear but it is not balanced. There are no clear advantages given and the answer does not use case studies or statistics. This answer achieves Level 2 but is limited to 9 marks because it is a one-sided argument.

Strong answer

Nuclear power stations produce electricity which carries on all the time, day or night, and provides the bulk of electricity for any country. At present in the UK there is a question over how we can produce enough electricity in the future. Fossil fuels may run out and are polluting and renewables are not thought to be able to produce enough power to sustain demand. Nuclear power is being run down and no new stations are being built so there was a question as to what would replace nuclear power. A good introduction, but would be better with an explanation of nuclear power too.

Nuclear energy has an advantage because it is cheap to produce once the power station is built. There are no fossil fuels involved so there is little carbon dioxide produced and there is a lot of uranium left. However, uranium is a non-renewable source of energy and the power stations are expensive to build, so it is not that clear cut. This is now a discussion, already putting both sides of an argument.

The big disadvantage with nuclear energy is the radioactive waste that is produced. This remains dangerous for thousands of years, meaning that land where it is stored cannot be used. The old reactors have to be encased in concrete and decommissioned at great expense so there is an economic cost here. ☞

Safety issues are also a problem and some have linked increased levels of cancer to this industry. There was widespread public distrust of nuclear power after the Chernobyl incident when radioactive rain fell on the UK. This needs more detail about Chernobyl.

The greatest advantage is that it can produce vast amounts of electricity from one power station and that this is constantly supplied and not dependent on the weather, like wind power would be. At this point some examples of countries which use nuclear power such as France and some statistics/facts would improve the answer.

In conclusion, nuclear power has many advantages for a steady source of power but there are safety issues, especially with radioactive waste. However, something will have to provide a lot of energy for the future and at present that might need to be nuclear power until we find a better alternative. This is a valid conclusion based on the evidence given with an opinion on the future.

This is a good answer but needs more detail and case studies. The impact of building new nuclear power stations and the NIMBY issues could be discussed as could better ways of storing used fuel and disposing of waste. A good Level 2 answer: 12 marks.

Health issues

Part (a)

Study figure 1, which shows the global morbidity of the infectious disease tuberculosis by country in 2008.

This question is point marked. Examiners are looking for descriptions of the global distribution. Global distributions can be described in terms of latitude or continents, but the simple naming of countries is not enough. A statement such as: 'All the countries in sub-Saharan Africa have over 100 new cases of TB per 100 000 ☞

of the population' is creditworthy, but to say 'Guyana, Surinam, Peru and Bolivia are all over 100 cases', is a list of countries and not worth a mark. Anomalies to the patterns are also worth a mark, e.g. 'Russia, Ukraine, Moldova and Romania are the only European countries with over 100 cases per 100000' is also worth a mark.

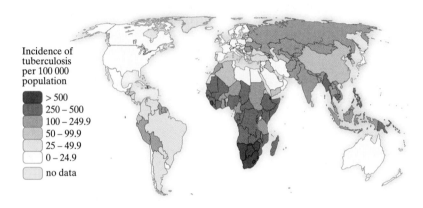

Fig. 1

Part (a) (i)

Describe the pattern shown in figure 1. [**4 marks**]

Average answer

Areas from the map which show a very little number of infectious diseases are mostly countries situated in the northern hemisphere such as Europe and the USA and also Australasia. Areas which have estimated cases of 300 or more are areas in the southern hemisphere and in less developed countries, particularly in sub-Saharan Africa and the odd parts of Asia.

2 marks: one for the N/S pattern and one for the point made about sub-Saharan Africa.

Strong answer

The pattern shown in figure 1 shows that areas such as the USA and many countries of Europe and Australia had very low occurrences of tuberculosis, with only an estimated 0–24 cases per 100 000 population. Other parts of the world, such as Africa for example, have very high occurrences of TB, with some countries having 300 or more cases per 100 000 people. Generally, countries above the Tropic of Cancer have low occurrences of TB but between the two tropics there are high occurrences of TB.

3 marks: one for the point made about the USA and Europe having low morbidity; one for recognizing that Africa has some countries with very high morbidity; one for recognizing the high incidence in the tropics.

Part (a) (ii)

Study figure 2 which shows the estimated maternal deaths from pregnancy-related causes by 2010. Examine the relationship between figure 1 and figure 2. [**6 marks**]

This answer is level-marked:
- **Level 1** will be awarded to answers that describe features on Figure 2 and/or make weak links with Figure 1.
- **Level 2** will be awarded for answers that relate to both Figures 1 and 2. Clear links have to be ☞

made between the patterns of maternal death and incidence of TB shown on maps. Candidates who put information into categories or provide evidence from figures 1 and 2 and/or assess the strength of those relationships with relevant comments will move to the higher part of the mark range.

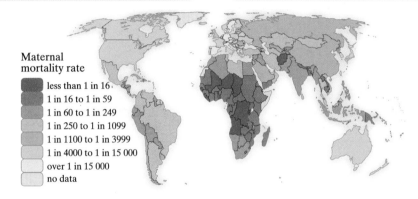

Maternal mortality rate

- less than 1 in 16
- 1 in 16 to 1 in 59
- 1 in 60 to 1 in 249
- 1 in 250 to 1 in 1099
- 1 in 1100 to 1 in 3999
- 1 in 4000 to 1 in 15 000
- over 1 in 15 000
- no data

Fig. 2

Average answer

The relationship between the figures is that countries with high occurrences of TB, such as those in Africa, have a high maternal mortality rate. This may be due to them being less developed so they do not have good healthcare available with medical advancements that will reduce the occurrence of TB and maternal mortality rates.

More developed countries such as the UK have low occurrences of TB and also low maternal mortality rates. This may be because the UK has good health facilities with education and knowledge on how to prevent such things occurring.

> There is a link made between the high TB morbidity and the maternal mortality with a weak attempt to link this with level of economic development. There is very little support. Level 1 would be awarded: 3 marks.

Strong answer

Figures 1 and 2 both show corresponding data relating to a country's economic growth and therefore healthcare. Again in Figure 2 you can see the highest cases of maternal mortality rate is in Africa, similar to the TB cases in Africa, they are both extremely high. Also other developing countries in Asia and South America have high maternal mortality rates (1 in 33 to 1 in 55) which also corresponds to their TB rates which were also high. Compare these figures with MEDCs in North America and Europe with both the lowest maternal mortality rates and TB cases. Figures 2 and 1 clearly show a relationship between the LEDCs having more cases of maternal mortality rates and TB cases and MEDCs barely suffering from these cases.

> There is a comparison between the TB morbidity and maternal mortality in Africa. This is followed by comments about Asia and South America. Comparisons are made between these and North America etc. There is an attempt to categorize. Level 2: 5 marks.

Part (b)

Choose one infectious disease. Outline the impact of this disease on the lifestyle of the people affected. **[5 marks]**

The mark scheme states that:

- **Level 1** will be given to answers that describe the impacts of their chosen disease, but in a random way. There will also be credit for any relevant general points made that have limited support.☞

- **Level 2** will be awarded to answers that show awareness of a variety of impacts and then categorize the impacts. The top of the level will be reached when specific points are made that have detailed support.

Average answer

One infectious disease could be HIV. It impacts on the lifestyle of the people affected because there is great stigma about people with HIV so people may be reluctant to talk about it in case people react against them. They have to be careful about transferring bodily fluids such as saliva and blood to others. Also pregnant mothers risk passing on HIV to their unborn child.

There are three impacts given, but no support. Level 1 awarded: 3 marks.

Strong answer

HIV, the virus which attacks the immune system and causes cell changes like cancer, causes AIDS which is an infectious disease which can be transferred by sexual intercourse, the sharing of needles, blood transfusions and from mother to child in pregnancy and which can affect the lifestyles of people. For example some people may be ashamed and not tell people about the disease because of the social stigma attached. In addition, if they're not careful they can pass the disease to new sexual partners unless they use condoms. Unborn babies that get the disease may die young or not get the opportunity to live their own life, without medication for the illness. Also, for example in Uganda where death rate from AIDS is high, many people die and leave orphaned children to look after themselves or are put in orphanages.

There is a wide range of impacts outlined: what HIV does to the immune system, social stigma, spreading infection, child deaths etc. However, the comments about how the disease is contracted are irrelevant. Level 2 awarded: 5 marks.

Part (c)

Discuss the impacts of obesity on people's health and the strategies that have been adopted to care for obese people. **[15 marks]**

The instruction to 'discuss' is one of the most common high-level command words. You are expected to build up an argument about this issue (obesity, its impacts and care strategies). You have to present more than one side of the argument and those arguments have to be supported by evidence. Examiners are not interested in your own personal opinion.

The extended prose mark scheme uses three level descriptors:

- At **Level 1** the answer describes the effects of obesity on people's health and/or care strategies. ☞

- At **Level 2**, the answer starts to develop the effects of obesity on people's health. It also starts to describe strategies to care for obese people and links healthcare strategies to causes of obesity. Arguments are supported and reference is made to relevant care strategies. The answer shows an element of discussion.

- At **Level 3**, there is a clear description of effects that obesity has on people's health. The answer is balanced and considers more than one strategy to care for obese people. Care for the obese is linked clearly to the causes of the problem. To get to this level the answer has to be precise and well structured with good support. There has to be discussion.

Average answer

Obesity greatly has an impact on people's health as they are more likely to suffer from type 2 diabetes, heart disease and things such as high cholesterol. General health is greatly reduced as exercise isn't regular and they may have more health problems. Despite some basic impacts, this introduction would have benefited from a definition of obesity.

Obesity would also be a drain on the NHS as they have to spend more time and money on problems caused by obesity and type of lifestyle.

There are more strategies to combat this though. Guildford for example is working with the Department of Transport to promote cycling – an active way of travelling to get people into shape and to take the strain off the NHS. A brief reference to a case study here which could have been developed in more detail.

There are also advertising strategies such as Change 4 Life which appears on adverts in an attempt to encourage people to change snacks, be more active and change their current way of life for a better one. ☞

At the moment now more than ever there is more focus on reducing obesity as we see a daily 'Get slim with GMTV' on in the mornings, and 'My Big Fat Diet Show' which has been on TV too. These aim to educate people about what they're consuming and encourage them to take part in physical activity so they can be happy with their way of life.

Finally nutritional information is now provided on most foods so people are aware of what they are eating and how good or bad it is for them. So, there are strategies available to encourage people to live a healthier way of life to reduce obesity.

There are a range of health effects mentioned, but very little support. The answer contains strategies, but simply names them rather than saying how they would be implemented. This answer would benefit from a case study of one health organization that has implemented strategies to help reduce obesity. Level 2 awarded: 10 marks.

Strong answer

Obesity is when someone is overweight and it is extremely damaging to their health. Obesity results in fats sticking to arteries which lead to the heart, resulting in the heart not receiving enough oxygen. This build-up of fat can lead to chronic heart disease which may lead to other health issues such as asthma or an individual may even have a heart attack. *This paragraph is a good introduction, with several clear impacts given but it could have been improved by a definition of obesity.*

Obesity affects people's health because they are unlikely to do any exercise. There is limited amount of oxygen reaching their heart so they become exhausted and will stop exercising. Obesity can also impact on people's fertility as they are less likely to conceive or will suffer complications during birth. Obesity affects every body system. *This paragraph contains several causes of obesity, which link into more impacts, and should form the basis of strategies to come.* ☞

Strategies adopted to care for people with obesity could be to promote healthy eating through advertisement or encouragement from different health professionals who may be helping a certain person overcome obesity.

There needs to be encouragement of exercise, e.g. some GPs offer free gym membership or free weeks at a weight watcher club such as Slimming World so people will be more likely to do something about it. There are also special classes available, especially for people who may be overweight so they won't feel self-conscious and they are more likely to go.

Government aims are to target obesity at an early age so it gives better and healthy lifestyles when they are older and increases people's life expectancy.

A range of health effects and strategies have now been given. There are links between the strategies and the causes of obesity. There has been no attempt to categorize the different impacts (e.g. health and lifestyle). There is limited support. This could have been improved by using a case study and assessing its success. Level 2: 12 marks.

Rivers, floods and management

Abrasion	The scraping, scouring, rubbing, grinding and drilling action of materials being moved by a river
Attrition	The collision of one piece of a river's load with another, breaking off bits of rock in the process. This has the effect of making the load rounder and smaller
Base level	The lowest limit to which erosion can take place, usually sea level
Braiding	This occurs when a heavily loaded river rapidly loses energy and rocks are deposited mid-channel
Channel cross profile	The view of a river channel from one side of the channel to the other
Cumec	The unit of discharge measured in $m^3\,s^{-1}$
Deforestation	The deliberate clearance of forest by cutting or burning
Deposition	The laying down of solid material, such as silt, on the river bed or flood plain
Drainage basin	The area of land drained by a river and its tributaries
Drainage basin hydrological cycle	An open system with inputs, outputs, transfers and stores that maps the movement of water through a drainage basin
Drilling	A form of abrasion where a pebble trapped in a hollow on a stream bed is rotated by the moving water so that it wears away the bedrock in a circular fashion
Efficiency	The ratio of the cross-sectional area of a river and its wetted perimeter. It is expressed as the hydraulic radius
Erosion	The wearing away of the land surface by rocks carried in a river
Evapotranspiration	The total amount of water leaving a vegetated surface by the joint processes of evaporation and transpiration
Graded profile	A theoretical form of river long profile that exists when there is a balance between the rate of erosion and the rate of deposition. Typically it is steep near the source and reduces in gradient towards the base level
Groundwater	Water which collects underground in pore spaces in rock
Groundwater flow	The movement of groundwater. This is the slowest transfer of water within the drainage basin. It provides water for the river during drought
Hard engineering	A series of management strategies where there is controlled disruption of natural processes by using man-made structures
Hjulstrom's curve	A graph that shows the relationship between the velocity of a river and the size of particles that can be eroded, transported and deposited
Hydraulic action	An erosion process where the banks and bed of the river are eroded by the moving water alone
Hydraulic radius	A measurement of the efficiency of a river; the ratio of the cross-sectional area of a river and its wetted perimeter

Infiltration	The movement of water from the surface downwards into the soil
Interception	The process by which precipitation is prevented from reaching the soil by leaves and branches of trees as well as by herbaceous plants and grasses
Kinetic energy	The energy of a moving mass. It is a function of mass and velocity
Long profile	A diagram that shows the changes in the altitude of a river's course as it goes from source to mouth
Overland flow	The rapid movement of water over saturated or impermeable land
Percolation	The downward movement of water from soil to the rock below or within rock
Potential energy	The energy stored in a mass as a result of its position in a force field (in this case, gravity)
Recurrence interval	The frequency with which a flood of given magnitude is likely to occur
Rejuvenation	An increase in the energy of a river as a result of a fall in base level or uplift of land
Roughness	A measurement of the frictional drag of a river bed on the moving water. It is calculated using the Manning's N formula
Runoff	All the water that flows out of a drainage basin
Saltation	A form of transportation where particles bounce along the river bed
Soft engineering	Ecologically sensitive management solutions to river erosion and flooding, e.g. afforestation or land-use zoning
Solution	A form of erosion where the river water dissolves soluble bedrock
Store	A part of the hydrological cycle where water stops moving. This can be either temporary or permanent
Storm hydrograph	A graph of river discharge in cumecs over the period of time from the onset of a rainstorm to when the river returns to its normal flow
Suspension	The transportation process whereby small material is carried in the body of a river
Thalweg	The part of the river that has maximum velocity and depth
Throughfall/stemflow	The water that drips off leaves or travels down the trunk of a tree during rainfall
Throughflow	The water that moves down-slope through soil
Traction	The rolling of river bedload along a river channel
Transportation	The movement of eroded particles from their origin to the place they are deposited
Valley cross profile	The shape of a river valley from one side of the valley to the other
Wetted perimeter	The total length of a river channel in cross section which is in contact with the water

Cold environments

Ablation (zone of)	The loss of ice from a glacier
Abrasion	The wearing away of rocks by ice using the debris it is carrying to drag along the surface
Accumulation (zone of)	The area where ice is gained to form glaciers
Arête	A sharp ridge made by two corries forming back to back
Bergschrund	A crevasse which forms where the ice starts to move away from the back wall of the corrie into the base of the hollow
Boulder clay (till)	Glacial moraine which has clay and stones in it
Blockfields	Large areas of big angular rocks
Cold/polar glaciers	Found in areas where the temperature rarely rises above freezing so there is little melting or movement
Compressing/ compressional flow	When ice crystals push together and compress so the ice becomes thicker with more erosion
Corrie (cirque or cwm)	An armchair-shaped hollow with a steep back wall formed by ice high up on a mountain side
Drumlins	Oval-shaped hills made of boulder clay. The long axis is parallel to the flow of the original glacier. The steep or stoss end faces to the direction of flow
Erratics	Large blocks of rock which were picked up and carried by a glacier or ice sheet and dropped a long way from their source
Esker	A long narrow ridge of glacial debris (mainly sand) which has been sorted by a stream that flowed beneath the glacier
Extending/ extensional flow	Occurs where the gradient increases and the velocity increases so that the ice becomes thinner and erosion is less
Freeze-thaw	A process that widens the joints in rocks through water expanding on freezing, then melting and collecting more water in the crack which then refreezes and cracks the rock open
Hanging valley	A valley which was a tributary valley entering the side of a glacial trough. The main valley was made deeper by the glacier but the side valley remained high above it
Ice cap	A dome-shaped mass of ice which develops on high plateaus
Ice sheet	Ice covering an area the size of a continent
Ice wedge	A crack in the ground caused by very cold temperatures which later fills with stones and gravels
Kame	A delta formed when meltwater from a glacier flows into a lake dammed up behind the terminal moraine down-valley

Kame terrace	Debris deposited by meltwater streams at the side of the glacier
Kettle holes	Occur where residual ice gets buried beneath lake sediment which protects it from heat and prevents it from melting. Eventually, on melting, a large depression is left
Moraine	Material eroded, transported and deposited by glaciers. There are several types dependent on their location: • **Lateral** – forms at the side of a glacier • **Medial** – forms along the middle of a glacier (from two lateral moraines in tributaries when the tributary joins the main valley) • **Terminal** moraine – collects at the end of the glacier • **Ground** moraine – forms beneath the glacier • **Englacial** moraine – moraine held within the glacier
Nivation	Where physical and chemical weathering under a patch of snow cause the rock to disintegrate
Outwash plain (sandur)	Downstream from the terminal moraine material is washed out in the meltwater and deposited on the flat plains
Patterned ground	This is material which is laid out on the surface and sorted by size by frost action in periglacial areas
Periglacial	Refers to areas near to ice sheets
Permafrost	Develops where soil stays frozen for two years. In the summer the surface layers usually melt, thawing from the surface downwards forming the active layer. There are several kinds: • **Continuous** permafrost – there is hardly any melting of the surface layer • **Discontinuous** permafrost – the permafrost is only up to 35 m deep and the surface melts in summer • **Sporadic** permafrost – the temperatures stay close to freezing and the permafrost is only found in cold spots
Piedmont glaciers	Formed where valley ice spreads out as it reaches lower areas
Pingos	These are dome-shaped features up to 50 m high formed by free water which refreezes and sediments are pushed up by hydrostatic pressure
Plucking	Ice freezes onto rocks. As the glacier pulls away the rocks are pulled with it
Push moraine	Formed where ice has re-advanced down the valley and pushed materials ahead of it
Pyramidal peak	A triangular-shaped peak formed where three corries meet back to back
Recessional moraine	Formed where the ice has retreated up-valley from the terminal moraine
Ribbon lake	Where there is an over-deepened section of the valley, or where there is softer rock which is more easily eroded, a rock basin forms which often fills with water
Roche moutonnée	An outcrop of resistant rock eroded by a glacier. The rocks are smooth on the up-valley side and plucked to form a jagged edge on the down-valley side.

Scree	Rocks which are angular and collect at the base of a slope
Solifluction lobes	Formed at the base of a slope where the active layer of material has gradually moved downwards over the summer and then refreezes in winter
Snout	The end of the glacier
Striations	Scratches in the surface of the rocks formed by stones embedded in the base of the ice as it moved over them so they are parallel to the direction of ice movement
Stone polygons/ stripes	Stones and boulders in a circular pattern on flat ground or striped pattern on a slope, caused by frost action
Surge	A sudden forward movement of a glacier
Thermokarst	Irregular landscape formed under periglacial conditions
Truncated spur	A river spur of a former river valley cut off by glaciation, leaving a steep cliff
Trough end	Found at the upper end of the valley where the glacier has entered from the corries above creating a steep wall
Tundra	Areas of the world which have permafrost and long cold winters limiting vegetation growth and life, e.g. northern Siberia and northern Canada
U-shaped valley (glacial trough)	The cross section of a glacial valley forms an open U shape with steep sides and a wide flat valley floor
Utilidor	A heated pipe for supplying water and oil and removing sewage and effluent in cold climates, which is insulated to prevent melting of the permafrost
Valley glacier	Where ice flows down a previously smaller (usually river) valley
Varves	Where there are layered deposits reflecting the seasonal flow of meltwater into lakes
Warm/temperate/ alpine glaciers	Found in areas where temperatures are high enough to cause some summer melting. This allows the glacier to move faster

Coastal environments

Abrasion (corrasion)	The waves carry sediments, especially sand and pebbles, which are thrown at the cliffs and wear them down
Attrition	Rocks are broken down into smaller particles by being knocked into each other by the waves and become more rounded
Arches	Where the sea breaks through the back wall of two caves which developed back to back in a headland
Barriers/dams/ barrages	Are built across river estuaries to control the flow of water
Bars	Form where a spit has stretched right across a bay or inlet often leaving a lagoon behind it. It can also refer to an offshore deposition

Beach cusps	Small curved hollows found on the beach
Beach replenishment	Artificially adding more beach materials to keep a beach in place
Berms	Ridges of materials on a beach caused by the action of the tide at its highest point
Blow holes	Formed where a crack at the back of a cave is opened up to the surface by wave action
Caves	These are developed on the coast where there is a joint or crack in the rock which is eroded by the action of the waves to form a large opening in the cliff
Constructive waves	These are waves which build beaches
Cost benefit analysis	Adding all the costs of a project and balancing it with all the benefits in money terms
Destructive waves	Waves which erode beaches and coasts
Eustatic	Global rise or fall in sea level
Fetch	The distance over which the wind has blown to produce waves
Freeze-thaw	Joints in rock collect water which freezes and expands, widening the joint. It then thaws, collects more water and freezes again expanding it and weakening it until the rock cracks
Gabions	Wire cages filled with rocks to protect against erosion
Groynes	Fences or low walls to prevent longshore drift
Hard engineering	Man-made structures used to control coastal processes
Headlands and bays	Where hard and soft rock alternate along a coastline, the softer rock will be eroded to form bays while the harder rock remains resistant to erosion and protrudes as a headland
Hydraulic action	This is where the force of the water in waves loosens material
Isostatic	Refers to a local change in sea level
Land use and activity management	Using regulations to limit building at the coast and to manage tourism
Longshore drift	The process by which material is moved along a beach
Managed retreat	Allowing some areas of the coastline to be breached by the sea in order to protect other areas
Neap tides	The lowest tidal range in any lunar month
Raised beaches	Produced where the land has risen above current sea level leaving an old beach stranded higher up on the cliffs
Revetment	A sloping concrete wall or wood structure to break up waves
Rias	A drowned river valley

Ridges and runnels	Alternating small ridges and dips found on beaches which run parallel to the shore line and are caused by strong backwash
Rip-rap (rock armour)	The building of various-shaped boulders which often lock together to break up the waves and protect the coast
Rotational slumping	Where a section of coast slumps into the sea in a concave action
Sand dunes	Where sand has been blown by the prevailing wind into large mounds along the coast
Salt marshes	Tidal, low-lying areas near the sea which have been colonized by salt-loving plants
Soft engineering	Uses natural materials and processes to help to protect the coastline
Solution (corrosion)	Where minerals in the rocks dissolve in water
Spits	These are long narrow stretches of sand or shingle which stick out into the sea and are formed by longshore drift
Spring tides	The highest tidal range in a lunar month
Stack	A small offshore island of rock created when an arch roof collapses
Storm beach	A high ridge at the back of the beach, built up by strong swash during spring tides and storms
Storm surge	A rise in sea level associated with very low pressure systems and high winds
Swash and backwash	With each wave the up-beach movement is called swash and the down-beach movement is backwash
Tidal range	The difference in height between high and low tides
Wave-cut platform	The rocky shoreline which is the base of the old cliffs, which have now been eroded further inland by wave action

Hot desert environments and their margins

Abrasion	An erosion process where sand, carried in suspension, is thrown against rocks and acts in a sandblasting fashion on those rocks
Arid	Describes an area that has less than 250mm of precipitation per year
Aridisol	The name for the soil commonly found in desert areas. Aridisols have a very low concentration of organic matter, reflecting the lack of vegetative production on these dry soils
Badlands topography	Landscapes that occur where softer sedimentary rocks and clay-rich soils have been extensively eroded by water and wind
Block separation	A mechanical weathering process that occurs on well-jointed and bedded limestones, where the rock breaks up into blocks along these weaknesses
Continentality	The influence of very large land masses on climate

Deflation	The removal of small-grained particles from an area by wind action
Deflation hollow	A depression in the desert floor created by deflation
Desertification	Land degradation in arid, semi-arid and dry sub-humid areas resulting from various factors, including climatic variations and human activities
Desert pavement or reg	A desert surface where the fine sand has been removed and a stony surface remains
Endoreic river	A river that flows into an inland drainage basin in the desert. E.g. the river Jordan
Ephemeral plants	Plants that grow for a short time only. Many desert plants are ephemeral as they grow only for brief periods after rain and then have a long dormancy phase
Ephemeral river	A river that flows intermittently, or seasonally, after rainstorms
Exfoliation	A weathering process where the outer layers of rock peel away like the layers of an onion
Exogeneous river	A river that originates from outside a desert. Many of these flow right through the desert and out into the sea. E.g. The river Nile
Food security/ insecurity	A concept referring to the availability of food and one's access to it
Frost shattering	A weathering process in jointed rock where temperatures fluctuate about 0C. It is the result of the alternating freezing and thawing of water and the resulting volume changes
Fuel wood	Wood is used in some developing countries as a fuel for cooking and heating
Granular disintegration	A weathering process where rocks break up grain by grain because of the differential expansion of different minerals
Overgrazing	This occurs when plants are exposed to intensive grazing for extended periods of time, or without sufficient recovery periods
Phreatophytes	These are deep-rooted plants that obtain most of the water they need from deep groundwater (the **phreatic zone**)
Rain shadow effect	The influence of a range of highland on the climate of the area downwind from it. Rain shadow areas tend to be very dry
Saltation	The process of transportation where sand grains are bounced along the surface by the wind
Semi-arid	An area where there is between 250mm and 500mm of rainfall per year
Surface creep	The process of transportation where sand grains are rolled along the surface
Suspension	The process of transportation where fine dust is picked up and carried by the wind
Tri-cellular model	A model that explains some of the main aspects of atmospheric circulation. It divides each hemisphere into three large convection cells

Xerophytes	Plants which are able to survive in an environment with little available water or moisture

Population change

Ageing population	This has a large number of older people in proportion to the working population
Agenda 21	This refers to the UN sustainable development programme but applied at a local level
Crude birth rate	This is the number of live births per thousand people per year
Crude death rate	This is the number of deaths per thousand people per year
Demographic Transition Model (DTM)	The model describes the change in the population of a country over time (or as a country develops economically)
Dependency ratio	The ratio of dependents to workers in a population
Doubling time	Refers to the expected time taken for a country's population to double
Fertility rate	This is the number of live births per thousand women aged 15–49 per year
Infant mortality rate	This is the number of children under the age of one who die per thousand live births per year
Juvenility index	This is the total population aged 0–19 divided by population over 20
Life expectancy	This is the average age to which a person is expected to live, at birth
Migration	This refers to people moving to a different location on a permanent basis
Natural increase rate	This is the crude birth rate *minus* crude death rate
Neo-Malthusians	Named after the pessimistic views of Malthus, they are theorists who predict that there will be a sudden decline in total population due to overuse of resources
Optimum population	This is where the resources available can be developed efficiently to satisfy the needs of the current population and provide the highest standard of living for a given level of technology
Overpopulation	This is where the population is too large for the resources available
Population density	This is the number of people living per unit area of land
Underpopulation	This exists where there are not enough people living in an area or country to utilize resources efficiently
Young population	This has a large number of younger people in proportion to the working population

Food supply issues

Appropriate/Inter-mediate technology	A range of simple technological innovations that have been designed for use in developing countries
Arable	Refers to the growing of crops
Capital	Money that is invested in soil improvement, machinery, buildings, pest control, high quality seeds/animals etc.
Carbon footprint	An estimate of how much carbon dioxide and other greenhouse gases an individual or organization produces and releases into the atmosphere
Cloning	The production of genetically identical organisms
Commercial	The production of crops or animal products for sale
Commercialization	The changing of an agricultural system from subsistence to commercial
Common Agricultural Policy (CAP)	An EU policy that aims to ensure reasonable prices for Europe's consumers and fair incomes for its farmers
Drip irrigation	A form of irrigation where water is directly applied to a plant or its roots
Environmental stewardship	A grant paid direct to a farmer regardless of how much he or she grows based on conservation and good environmental practice
European Union	An economic and political union of 27 states throughout Europe
Extensive	Farming that is carried out on a large scale over a large area
Food and Agriculture Organization (FAO)	A United Nations agency with responsibility for agriculture, forestry, fisheries and rural development
Food miles	The number of miles food travels from where it is produced to where it is consumed
Food security	When all people at all times have access to sufficient, safe, nutritious food to maintain a healthy and active life
Genetic modification (GM)	The process of taking genes from one species and adding them to the DNA of another species
Geopolitics	A description of how countries interact with each other and the spatial implications of this
Green Revolution	A series of new agricultural techniques that have brought about increases in food production in developing countries
High yield variety (HYV)	New crop varieties that have been developed to produce high yields per hectare
Intensive	High output per hectare based on high inputs of capital or labour
Intervention price	An EU policy that guaranteed farmers a reasonable price for their produce whether it could be sold on the open market or not

Land colonization	The movement of people onto previously uninhabited and uncultivated land
Land reform	A government-imposed change in land ownership. Large, often absentee landlords are replaced by smaller owner-occupier farmers
Livestock	Domestic animals kept for meat or dairy production
Mixed farming	The growing of crops and the raising of livestock all on the same farm
Quota	An EU-imposed restriction on the quantity of particular agricultural products farmers were allowed to sell
Set-aside	An EU policy that obliged farmers to leave a percentage of their land uncultivated
Subsidy	Financial support given to farmers by the EU intended to maintain income stability
Subsistence	The description of a farming system where farmers produce enough to feed themselves and their family
Tariff	A tax levied on imports or exports
Transnational corporation (TNC)	The name for a company that operates in more than one country
World Trade Organization (WTO)	A global international organization dealing with the rules of trade

Energy issues

Acid rain	Rain which has become more acidic than normal from mixing with pollutants such as sulphur dioxide and nitrogen oxides, caused by the burning of fossil fuels
Appropriate intermediate technology	This refers to technology which is suited to the area where it is to be used. It is often locally made and low cost
Biofuels	Where biomass is used to produce energy, e.g. fuel wood and sugar cane
Carbon credits	Units of measurement for carbon offsets (when businesses have reduced their carbon emissions). They can then be used for carbon trading
Carbon trading	Where a country or company which has met its targets for carbon dioxide reduction, gains carbon credits, which it can sell to another company or country
Energy conservation	Refers to the attempts to reduce energy use and prevent waste, to slow down global energy consumption
Energy mix	This refers to the combination of energy resources used to provide energy for a country at a certain time
Fossil fuels	Energy sources which were formed millions of years ago and are not being replaced: coal, oil and gas

Geopolitics	The study of the relationship between politics, geography and economics, especially related to a country's foreign policy and development of resources
Global warming	Relates to the theory of climate change seen as a result of increasing temperatures due to increased greenhouse gas production from burning fossil fuels
Low carbon vehicles	Vehicles that produce less carbon dioxide than petrol or diesel vehicles. They include electric cars, hybrids and those powered by LPG (liquefied petroleum gas)
Non-renewable resources	These are finite resources which will run out
Primary energy resources	Energy in its raw form which has not been refined or changed
Renewable resources	These are resources which will not run out and are continuously available
Secondary energy resources	This is energy converted form a primary source into a more useful form, e.g. coal to electricity
Sustainable development	Providing for current demand for energy without adversely affecting the supplies for the future
Tidal barrage	A dam built across a tidal estuary in order to use the power of the tide to generate electricity
Transnational corporation (TNC)	The name for a company that operates in more than one country

Health issues

Age structure	This refers to the proportion of people in different age groups within a population. Common descriptions of population age structures are youthful and ageing
Anopheles mosquito	The species of mosquito where the female acts as the vector of the disease, carrying the plasmodium from victims of malaria to previously uninfected people
Antimalarial drugs	Drugs designed to either prevent a person from contracting malaria or to cure the disease
Artemisinin-based therapies	These are a group of drugs that possess the most rapid action of all current drugs against certain forms of malaria. Use of the drug by itself is discouraged by the World Health Organization as there have been signs that malarial parasites are developing resistance to the drug
Branded drug	A branded drug has a trade name, is manufactured by a well-established pharmaceutical company, and protected by a patent. It cannot be produced or sold by any other company. A brand name will be simpler than the generic name
Case mortality rate (C-MR)	The number of people dying from a disease divided by the number who have that disease
Crude death rate	The number of deaths in one year per thousand of a population

Disability adjusted life year (DALY)	A measure of overall disease burden, expressed as the number of years lost due to ill-health, disability or early death
Essential drugs	These are generic drugs that can provide safe and effective treatment for a variety of common but serious health complaints
Famine	A chronic shortage of food in which many people die of starvation
Generic drug	A drug which is produced and distributed without patent protection. They tend to be cheaper than branded versions of the same drug
Global Malaria Programme	This programme is responsible for malaria surveillance, monitoring and evaluation, policy and strategy formulation, technical assistance, and coordination of WHO's global efforts to fight malaria
Infant mortality rate	The number of deaths of infants under one year old per thousand live births
Infectious diseases	These are caused by pathogenic microorganisms, such as bacteria, viruses, parasites or fungi; the diseases can be spread, directly or indirectly, from one person to another
Life expectancy	The average number of years at birth that a person can be expected to live
Malnutrition	Lack of adequate nutrition caused by an unbalanced diet
Morbidity	This refers to the prevalence of illness or disease. It can be measured by DALYs
Mortality	The death of people. It is measured by a number of indices including death rate and infant mortality
Non-communicable disease	A disease which is not contagious. Risk factors such as a person's lifestyle, genetics, or environment are known to increase the likelihood of certain non-communicable diseases
Premature death rate	This is defined in the UK as the number of deaths of people under the age of 65 per 1 000 of the population
Primary Care Trust (PCT)	A type of NHS trust, part of the National Health Service in England, that provides some primary and community services or commissions them from other providers
Transnational corporation (TNC)	A company which has bases in more than one country
Vector-borne disease	This is a disease in which the microorganism causing the disease is transmitted from an infected individual to another individual by an insect or other agent
World Health Organization (WHO)	This is the directing and coordinating authority for health within the United Nations system. It is responsible for providing leadership on global health matters

Index